The Definitive Guide to Buying Legal Services

Dr. Silvia Hodges Silverstein (Editor)

Haley Crain Carter, Pamela Cone, Stephanie Corey, Dr. Orazio Difruscolo, Sandy Duncan, Adrienne Fox, Steph Hogg, Kelly Hotchkiss, Anja Jähnel, Susan Krasaway, Tina Ksienzyk, Caroline O'Grady, Richard Stock, Yannis Theile, Nick Williams, Jason Winmill, and Lynsey Wood

Buying Legal® Council

www.buyinglegal.com

2021

Published by the Buying Legal® Council.

www.buyinglegal.com

Published in 2021.

Publisher's Note
This publication is designed to provide accurate and authoritative information in regard to the subject matter covered. It is sold with the understanding that the publisher is not engaged in rendering legal, accounting or other professional services. If you require legal advice or other expert assistance, you should seek the services of a competent professional.

ISBN: 9798579769718

Printed in the United States of America.

Cover design by Buying Legal® Council.
Cover photo by Lindsey Middleton (Unsplash.com).

For MJS, John, Mami & Papi.

The Definitive Guide to Buying Legal Services is dedicated to the "father of legal procurement", Marty Harlow. His trailblazing work has single-handedly changed this industry as well as the lives of those that have worked with him and for him.

May you enjoy your retirement. Go boating, throw a whopper plopper, and bake bread and cookies.

We're forever grateful and miss you!

ABOUT THE BUYING LEGAL® COUNCIL

The Buying Legal® Council is the international trade organization for professionals tasked with sourcing legal services and managing supplier relationships.

We are the only organization focused on buying legal services, alternative, ancillary legal services and legal technology. Come to us for the latest thinking and most up-to-date best practices and research.

MEMBERSHIP: For client-side professionals. You work in procurement, operations, or in the legal department and are tasked with buying legal, alternative, ancillary legal services and/or legal technology.

FRIENDSHIP: For supplier-side professionals. You work in marketing/business development/sales or provide, consult and/or sell legal services, alternative, ancillary legal services and/or legal technology.

Why Join Us?

Access the largest knowledge base on buying legal services best practices.

Benefit from the insights and experience, and be a part of the community!

Onboarding Fast & Easy: How you handle the first 100+ days in the legal category will be crucial for your success as it sets the tone for building the necessary trust with your colleagues as well as the providers of legal services.

- ☑ Follow our Ten Steps To Success Onboarding Process to get the skills necessary to advance your career.
- ☑ Get your Certificate Fundamentals of Legal Procurement.

Continued Education: Strengthen your knowledge and skills with our Continued Education program. You will have access to the latest thinking and best practices on buying legal, alternative legal, and ancillary legal services, and legal technology. Our educational material will make you even more successful at your job.

- ☑ Best Practices Webinars
- ☑ Expert and Peer-to-Peer Roundtables

Access Best Practices: As the only organization dedicated to buying legal services, alternative, and ancillary legal services as well as legal technology, you can benefit from the many best practice materials available to you. Find solutions for your legal procurement issues and learn from the insights from your peers and experts.

- ☑ High impact Cheat Sheets & Checklists
- ☑ Deep-insight Primers
- ☑ Templates
- ☑ Best practices Videos
- ☑ Best practices Slides
- ☑ "Mini Law School" Legal Lessons

Gain Insights: Our Market Intelligence Report Legal is the most comprehensive legal category report of its kind. For Members and Friends, it is free of charge.

- ☑ Access our Masterclasses and Bootcamps on Pricing Legal Services
- ☑ Access conference materials and slide decks

Engage with your Peers: Build your career and engage with your peers on matters that are important to you. Join our Working Groups or start your own.

- ☑ Diversity & Inclusion
- ☑ Social Impact & Sustainability

Get Discounts: Members and Friends benefit from exclusive discounts on Buying Legal© Council events as well as discounts and exclusive offers from our partners.

Please visit **www.buyinglegal.com** for more information.

TABLE OF CONTENTS

FOREWORD
PROFESSOR STEPHEN MAYSON

The way in which legal services are bought in the 21st century continues to be transformed. The increased buying power and sophistication of clients and consumers in all market segments and geographies places a premium on understanding their motivation and decision-making. In some cases, the disconnection between lawyer and prospective client created by formalised procurement processes exacerbates the difficulties of pitching for new work.

It is not that the age of the 'trusted adviser' is behind us, but the idea of selling time and seniority founded on longstanding personal relationships is certainly no longer the predominant model. The effect on legal practice of the twin paradigm - shifters of technological advance and a global pandemic - signal further uncertainty and challenge.

As with the *Legal Procurement Handbook* [published in 2015], this book offers a wealth of insights into how the buying and procurement process is conceived and managed, and therefore what might be more effective. Now, more than ever, anyone involved in buying or selling legal services must read it.

Professor Stephen Mayson
London, UK

FOREWORD
TOM SAGER

Dr. Silverstein deserves another "job well done" in drawing upon the considerable expertise and talent of this amazing group of procurement professionals. Thanks to her leadership and vision, the world of procurement in the legal profession has advanced dramatically. *The Definitive Guide to Buying Legal Services* is exceptionally well organized and captures succinctly the successful strategies, approaches, insights, and everyday practice tips that will serve our profession for years to come.

But what will really enable this resource to become an indispensable tool for the in-house lawyer will largely depend upon the recognition by the General Counsel of the importance of developing a highly collaborative process with other like-minded lawyers, both inside and outside, and with knowledgeable ancillary suppliers within her organization and beyond.

Few other disciplines, like the world of procurement, require such a diverse mix of talent to insure the appropriate segmentation of legal service providers that will deliver creative pricing and efficiency tools which are market facing and will provide competitive advantage. And this must be done through a careful vetting process to insure that the legal function's team of procurement professionals are treated as equals with each role being well defined and embraced.

The end result with the aid of this treatise should be a dedicated group of law firms and providers that are aligned, focused on the core objectives, accountable, trust worthy and transparent. Having worked for DuPont for 38 years as an in-house lawyer and ultimately General Counsel, I realize now that we failed to recognize the importance of a disciplined procurement process. Now with the assistance of talented and savvy in-house professionals and a network of lawyers, IT professionals and others who are truly committed to advancing the best interest of their client, dramatic improvement in the results are doable using this resource tool. Having retired from DuPont and then joining Ballard Spahr, I have observed first hand how a successful collaboration with the right professionals can deliver great value. And, reliance upon *The Definitive Guide to Buying Legal Services* will only accelerate the transformation.

Tom Sager
Philadelphia

INTRODUCTION TO THE BOOK

Buying legal services should be part of your organization's procurement department responsibilities. If you have not yet gotten involved, this is your invitation to do so as it is best practice today. For many companies, it is an untapped source of incremental savings and improvement in efficacy.

The legal category has some specific nuances and unique challenges that you want to be aware of, but the principles that apply to buying other complex and professional services also apply to buying legal services. Handle your organization's legal procurement needs carefully, just like other areas of spend where getting it wrong could be very costly to your organization – think IT.

The Definitive Guide to Buying Legal Services will guide you on how to take the best approach to buying legal services and technology for the legal department (aka "legal tech"). Learn from the experience of others and understand what works and what does not. After reading the Guide, you will be aware of leading practices and can apply them to your organization so you can be even more successful. The legal category is a special challenge as many lawyers are still not used to the benefits of a robust procurement approach. Advocate the benefits and value of a structured procurement approach and get their buy-in. It allows for a wider and more open conversation with stakeholders about value and delivery, or performance management of suppliers (law firms included).

In the following chapters, *The Definitive Guide to Buying Legal Services* will explore the different aspects of best practice legal services buying. We wish you much success in the legal category and when buying legal services. We welcome your feedback and input for future editions. Thank you and best of luck!

The co-authors
Haley Crain Carter, Pamela Cone, Stephanie Corey, Dr. Orazio Difruscolo, Sandy Duncan, Adrienne Fox, Steph Hogg, Kelly Hotchkiss, Anja Jähnel, Susan Krasaway, Tina Ksienzyk, Caroline O'Grady, Richard Stock, Yannis Theile, Nick Williams, Jason Winmill, Lynsey Wood, and editor Dr. Silvia Hodges Silverstein

A heartfelt "Thank you" to:
- BTI Consulting, Elevate, Lawcadia, and Wolters Kluwer's ELM Solutions for your expertise and insights
- Lorenzo Berenguer, Jo Ellen Hatfield, Andie Lam, Simone Claudia, and Doria Delgado-Thompson for proofreading, commenting, and supporting
- Jennifer Black-Sherman, Laura Buliga, Pamela Cone, Orazio Difruscolo, Laura Doyle, Sandy Duncan, Adrienne Fox, Marty Harlow, Jo Ellen Hatfield, Janes Isles, Andy Krebs, Tina Ksienzyk, Andie Lam, Jon Lane, Paul Lewis III, Denise Liddy, Milly Parekh, and Jessica Williams for your continuous support and time as board members or working group leaders

Please note that the information contained in this Guide reflects the personal views and experience of the authors and not of their respective employers.

GET READY FOR BUYING LEGAL SERVICES

Over the last decade, many organizations have started to professionally manage legal spend with the help of procurement. Large banks, insurance companies, pharmaceutical companies and other buyers of legal services have been at the forefront of this development. Before Procurement's involvement, the "traditional" approach to buying legal services typically was a two-tier process. In-house lawyers based their choice of outside counsel on the type, scope, scale, and importance of a given matter or legal issue. They may have considered whether a provider was the right type of firm for example, for high-stakes litigation or for a large volume due diligence exercises. Did these firms have the appropriate competence and reputation? Once in-house counsel were clear about the "tier" of firm needed, they would consider which lawyer or lawyers they had good experience with in the past. Here, the selection was mostly about personality, chemistry, the right fit, relationships, trust, and word of mouth.

The new "Procurement" approach to buying legal services, is based on a more objective choice of legal service provider tier: Can the firm or provider do the work? Procurement, working with Legal, will conduct market analysis, due diligence on law firms and other legal services providers to assess and evaluate them. In a second step, Procurement will look at data and benchmarks to assist Legal with a more metrics-driven, auditable choice of firm or provider.

It is often top management that brings in Procurement with the mandate to:

(1) Support the legal department to (better) manage legal spend
(2) Find more effective ways to negotiate with law firms and other legal services providers
(3) Develop a more efficient purchasing process management
(4) Measure best value from law firms and other legal services providers
(5) Conduct more objective comparisons of law firms and other legal services providers

Procurement is typically responsible for:
- Framework agreements
- Pricing negotiations
- Influencing which firms to select
- Overseeing due diligence activities
- Negotiating the terms and conditions (T&Cs)
- Controlling the selection process
- Engagement letter/retainer

Your sourcing strategy should not reinvent the wheel but use tried and tested best practice methodologies, tailored to your organization. It should be constructive, measured, and appropriate. A sourcing approach that is based on a clearly defined strategy and vision can deliver significant business benefits to your organization, including total cost of ownership (TCO) savings, service level enhancement, technology transformation, best-practice governance and business agility. TCO is a calculation method that determines the overall cost of a product or service throughout its life cycle. This method combines both direct and indirect costs.

It is unlikely to be all about bottom-line savings or cost mitigation as for example, reducing the level of legal risk or shortening a product life cycle could be worth many times more to an organization than the reduction in the cost of a piece of legal advice.

Any sourcing category plan you put together needs to be based on profound knowledge of the overall supply market as well as of sub-markets and this is no different for legal. The legal marketplace covers a whole spectrum of activities from the provision of legal advice via traditional law firms, so-called alternative legal service providers or law companies, technology-driven legal solutions, and legal process outsourcing to a range of ancillary services that support legal processes, including 'on-demand' contingent legal resources.

One of your most important tasks, and potentially the most challenging, is matching your organization's legal services requirements or business needs to the marketplace offerings. You need to determine these needs within the context of your organization's strategic objectives and priorities to ensure that your sourcing approach is properly aligned. Other considerations need to include the extent to which the buying organization wants to align itself with culturally "fit" supply partners to drive wider agendas, such as inclusion and diversity or sustainability and social impact.

As with all supply markets there are always changes as a result of new market entrants, technological developments and changes to regulations etc. Historically, legal services providers have not been the most dynamic of supply markets but the speed of change appears to be increasing and the legal buyer needs to be cognizant of this. Because of the complexity of legal services, robust knowledge and experience in the category is key to success.

Your sourcing strategy should incorporate all of the elements that lead-up to the purchase of all types of legal services.

With the legal category in particular, try not to jump in too fast to get involved with live projects straight away unless you have some knowledge and can do so in tandem and without diverting your attention. If you are only involved in the legal category for a short time, parachuted in for an 18 to 24-month assignment supporting Legal with a light touch, this will not be sufficient to increase your ability to do this matching or even contribute in a meaningful way to the sourcing discussion internally or externally with the firms and providers.

Experience shows that tenure has great influence on a Legal Procurement professional's success. So be patient and aim to become part of this industry. Get to know your colleagues in the legal department and develop relationships of trust.

In the legal category, requests for proposal (RFPs) are typically used to establish a preferred roster of panel firms, to generally assess providers' capabilities, establishing appropriate fee arrangements, agreed billing guidelines, etc. or for individual matters, or to sole source a region or category of work. Prior involvement in the strategy behind that review, the reasoning and selection criteria and the work that follows, however, are even more important. Your legal procurement strategy should help you:

- ☑ Manage the long-term requirement for services
- ☑ Deeply analyze your business needs
- ☑ Research and develop your understanding of the marketplace

- ☑ Employ data to assist with decision making
- ☑ Define the best price for a particular service
- ☑ Consider multiple factors such as optimal relationships
- ☑ Reduce long-term risks
- ☑ Include technology such as the employment of applications or automation elements

Now let us dive into your own Legal Procurement adventure!

DESIGN A SOURCING STRATEGY

Your first step will need to be designing a sourcing strategy for legal services and legal tech. It will help you formalize your way of working and show to your colleagues in the legal department that you are worth involving. The consolidated purchasing power that a strategy will bring carries weight with senior management to make a difference and to ensure that a clear and concise, collaborative document acts as a solid plan. It will also help you align with the long-term goals of your organization, bear in mind external as well as internal factors, and have an eye on the total cost of ownership rather than just the price.

When done well, your sourcing program for legal services should describe your organization's non-financial objectives, the optimal configuration of primary and secondary firms by jurisdiction, reporting and billing requirements, and the place of technology to improve effectiveness and efficiency. It should also set financial targets for total legal spend and for savings to be achieved, your organization's objectives for non-hourly pricing, annual pricing increases, disbursements, law firm performance, annual review and adjustment mechanisms, and payment terms.

Before you can do this, you will need to start by understanding the status quo. Gather as much data and information as you can about how your organization has been buying legal services so far and what has been done before. Try to understand the reasons behind the choices. Probe on what works well and why, as well as what did not work so well. Get a good understanding of who is in control and how. Spend data is a key reference point for all procurement professionals. Legal spend data might seem somewhat straightforward at a first look – you may find that the billing data you collect is very insightful and allows you to analyze usage to a high degree – but in all likelihood, you will soon notice that it will take you more time and effort to understand all the details. Legal services tend to be rather opaque in billing unless clients request transparent invoices.

Remain curious and be inquisitive about everything, particularly the data. Ask questions such as:
- Why was a particular firm chosen?
- Why was a particular fee earner used for this matter?
- Why do the fee earners get charged at a this hourly rate?
- Why does it take a specific amount of time to do the work?

Getting to the stage where you understand this decision-making in detail will help you understand how your organization operates. It is critical that you understand how you can align your organization's overall business goals to your legal services sourcing strategy. Your organization's business goals should inform all plans and business decisions. If the goal is, for example, "To achieve consistent year-on-year revenue growth of at least 10 percent," your sourcing strategy needs to show precisely how you interpreted this in your sourcing strategy and how your strategy will contribute. Putting your strategy into the wider context of what your organization is trying to achieve will put you in a much stronger position when you ask your stakeholders to sign-off on your plan. You will also have a much more coherent message for the marketplace once you start to engage it. From a firm or provider perspective, they like nothing less than a narrow-minded approach that focuses on one element only – costs. If you want to engage firms and providers, include options for them to show how their services may be able to reduce time, increase quality, show technology-based advantage etc.

STRATEGIES TO SOURCE LEGAL SERVICES

To prepare your strategies to source legal services (aka your legal vendor strategy), undertake a robust business requirement gathering exercise. Look at both supply risk and financial risk. The Kraljic Matrix and related models help identify different strategies you should apply under different circumstances. For example, in areas where availability is limited and costs are high (such as for specialist mergers and acquisitions activity) you may need a strategic sourcing strategy. For non-critical routine areas (such as employee contracts, where many law firms have the relevant skillsets), you would want to take a different approach and opt for a cost-focused strategy.

When buying legal services, you have a number of sourcing strategies that you can apply. Let us explore a number of options, outlining the key benefits and disadvantages of each strategy. Please do keep in mind that this is of course a more generic approach to strategy development and that other factors may come into play, such as:

- Your organization's risk appetite towards the use of external providers
- Your organization's attractiveness as a client/customer
- The capability of your in-house legal team
- Geography (It may not be cost effective for a global organization to have providers in every territory)
- Cost (Legal budgets may influence the extent to which your organization engages legal services providers)
- Preference (In-house counsel often determine which firms or legal services providers will be used based on professional preference)

- Diversity of requirements (It is not possible nor cost effective to have a team of lawyers available for every possible scenario)
- Ease of doing business with (Both your organization and your firms or legal services providers)
- Other external factors (such as social pressure to engage in sustainable procurement)

| Bottleneck | Strategic |
| Non-critical | Leverage |

Supply risk (vertical axis) — Financial risk (horizontal axis)

KRALJIC MATRIX

Let us consider possible strategies you may wish to pursue for engaging external lawyers for advisory services:

FIRM-CENTRIC LEGAL PANEL

Setting up a firm-centric legal panel is one of the most commonly used approaches for buying legal services. Establishing a panel of external counsel based on a law firm's capability assumes that the firm has sufficient breadth and depth of expertise and is not dependent on a small number of individuals. Your panel may consist of a mix of multi-service law firms or of firms that specialize in (a) particular area(s).

This approach is particularly effective where the work is straightforward, of substantial volume or the firm itself is seen as a specialist in a certain practice area, geography etc.

You should carefully consider your panel structure to avoid compromising quality. You should also have an off-panel process in case your panel firms do not have the necessary expertise or are conflicted out.

Benefits	Disadvantages
• You are able to develop strategic relationships with firms (particularly where volume/spend is present) • Your firm becomes familiar with your organization's approach, potentially reducing costs • You have the opportunity to have a panel-wide approach • You have the ability to standardize instructions	• It can be less effective where spend/volumes are lower • You need to invest in vendor panel management • It may not be possible to manage all your external work through your panel

and matter management processes • You have access to (free) added-value services such as Secondments, training, bulletins etc. • You have a greater opportunity to implement e-billing and bill review procedures • You are more likely to embed values in the supply chain such as sustainability	

A panel based on individual lawyers' expertise (rather than the firms they work for) is particularly beneficial where specialist advice is required. It also complements a fully resourced in-house legal department that does most of the work in-house.

Benefits	Disadvantages
• You have access to required expertise for the specific instruction • This approach works better where there is no material volume and you still want access to leading lawyers (specific lawyers are hired for certain matters) • It requires less time and cost spent on panel management	• Your organization is less likely to benefit from e-billing and bill review • You will likely pay a premium for those lawyers (higher hourly price) • Your cost of governance and compliance may increase, particularly if lawyers move firms • You are less likely to be able to embed consistency

In practice, the lawyer-centric legal panel approach is rare. Most organizations will implement a combined approach depending on the specific requirements. For example, an insurance company may have a panel of law firms for straightforward automotive claims, but may need specific lawyers for advice on complex aviation claims. Similarly, the volume in one country or jurisdiction could warrant a firm-centric legal panel approach, but use a more ad-hoc approach in other countries or jurisdictions.

AD-HOC APPOINTMENTS/INSTRUCTION-BASED SOURCING

Appointing lawyers on an ad-hoc or per case basis is the appropriate strategy when demand for legal advice is limited. This is typical for smaller organizations, those with limited requirements for (certain types of) legal services or when conflicts arise with panel firms.

Benefits	Disadvantages
• This approach is appropriate where the requirement for legal advice is minimal • It minimizes time and cost spent on vendor management	• Relationships and knowledge of the market may be lost • (Lack of) Speed: This approach will require time for sourcing and onboarding law firms and other legal services providers which may be a challenge when an instruction is urgent

PURCHASING CONSORTIUM

Purchasing Consortiums increase your buying power by pooling different organizations' demands to collectively purchase goods or services. As the contract becomes more lucrative, law firms and other legal services providers may be more likely to offer added benefits, invest in relationship management, and focus on providing a service to retain the business in the future.

Benefits	Disadvantages
• Your organization benefits from wider expertise of the legal market • Your consortium's combined spend results in stronger buying power • You gain access to (more) competitive rates, added value and relationship management • You can share governance and compliance activities	• The consortium approach may require a decision-by-committee to avoid conflict which can result in compromising your own business requirements • It is less flexible if your own business requirements change • This approach may result in larger spend organizations in your consortium driving the decisions • It is possible that law firms and legal services providers will give some organizations preferential treatment • This approach is typically tied into a pre-agreed time period

VENDORS OFFERING WIDER LEGAL SERVICES (ONE-STOP SHOP)

Organizations will often seek to partner with law firms and legal services providers that go beyond traditional advisory and litigation services. These providers effectively become a one-stop shop for legal and related ("ancillary") services. Examples include e-discovery, court reporting, legal training, recovery, or witness assessment. This is a form of 'bundling' procurement.

Benefits	Disadvantages
• It gives you the opportunity to leverage spend • You will have fewer firms and providers to onboard and manage	• Quality may be compromised unless key performance indicators (KPI) are set up that guard against this • A formal engagement will likely require that terms and conditions are recorded in a comprehensive contractual agreement (e.g. delivery standards, penalty clause, data security, etc.)

Some organizations may choose to combine purchasing power for different types of legal and non-legal services and seek providers that can deliver all of those services. Alternative legal service providers, also known as law companies, is an umbrella term including any business providing certain types of legal services without being a law firm. For example, the 'Big Four' firms have diversified into legal services in many jurisdictions, offering those alongside other advisory services. This is also a form of 'bundling' procurement.

Benefits	Disadvantages
• This approach gives you the opportunity to leverage spend • Potential backing of larger providers for investment in technology	• This type of provider is not permitted/offered in all jurisdictions • The selection process may be more difficult to assess • Quality may be compromised

Another strategy is to outsource legal processes to third parties from the entire function to certain aspects such as corporate management (e.g. company secretarial services), contractual work or specific business functions. Legal Process Outsourcing is the application of Business Process Outsourcing to the legal function.

Benefits	Disadvantages
• This approach reduces organization overhead • It providers you access to a full suite of legal services • Flexible model to accept additional workload	• Need to ensure that appropriate oversight is in place • You would not be able to rely solely on the outsourced provider • Lack of control • Requires audit services where outsourcing is substantial

Partial outsourcing can be a cost-effective way of reducing the work of the legal department ensuring that the right activities are performed by the most appropriate resource. Routine contracts or vendor bill review could be undertaken by third parties who have the right level of resource and expertise to complete the task.

From a control environment standpoint, the higher the degree of outsourcing, the higher the need for a systematic and disciplined approach to ensure that services are being delivered as expected.

In-house legal departments increasingly engage flexible resources they can deploy as and when required: The client contacts the provider with requirements and receives details of lawyers, paralegals, or other personnel that fit the requirements and are available for work.

Benefits	Disadvantages
• This can be a cost-effective solution to resourcing as it removes the need to retain staff • You gain access to a wider variety of immediately available expertise • It is suitable for routine requirements • Vendors can even manage projects on your behalf	• The expertise you require may not be readily available • Your organization may face challenges regarding the consistency of the lawyers provided • Retaining staff on your projects can be a challenge if they are offered permanent positions elsewhere • Knowledge of the organization is limited

It is important to distinguish this concept from outsourcing the legal department in its entirety. This option is purely designed to accommodate resourcing constraints and is not designed to replace the function.

In many organizations, the legal department upskills internal business areas to deal with routine legal work themselves. This is particularly common for contract work where the legal department creates templates, which other departments or business units themselves can use. Examples would be self-service vendor contracts for Procurement or employee contracts for Human Resources. This benefits both sides – the legal department frees up resources and the departments or business units avoid a possible time bottleneck created by Legal.

CHECKLIST:
- ☑ Align your sourcing strategies with your organization's overall/business strategy and risk appetite
- ☑ Depending on the need and your organizational culture and preferences, you may want to combine different approaches of sourcing strategies
- ☑ Regularly review your sourcing strategy

SECURE SPONSORSHIP

The stakeholders affected by strategic sourcing for legal services can be numerous and varied even within an organization. Many departments or business units require external legal services. Some will require them occasionally and others on a systematic and regular basis. A successful sourcing program goes beyond managing a process efficiently in order to save on legal costs. To truly secure stakeholder sponsorship, it must actively engage primary and secondary stakeholders at key intervals.

Securing sponsorship means getting the approval and active support for a formal program that will achieve specific qualitative and financial results for the company. Documenting the terms of such an undertaking should take the form of a written proposal and can then serve as an anchor and a point of reference for the Project Manager. "Securing sponsorship" should result in "An Agreement to Source Efficient and Effective External Legal Services." This suggests that Procurement is an equal stakeholder and must be on an equal footing with Legal as the primary stakeholders.

WHO ARE THE STAKEHOLDERS

Over the last 20 years, general counsel have been held uniquely accountable for the quality of legal services used by their companies, even if they do not manage all legal fees in a central budget. Human Resources, Compliance, Claims, Commercial Lending, Research and Development and other departments or business units often work with their own roster of external counsel and may even have their own budgets. Legal fees could be charged to the department or business unit at year-end, to a specific transaction, or to the clients of the organization.

Another critical internal stakeholder and service partner is IT, as it possesses critical skills to e.g., extract data from key systems, develop new reports, improve existing reports, conduct data cleanup etc. Their requirements are varied and it is important that these are considered by engaging the appropriate stakeholders in the review.

While these are important stakeholders, they are not in a position to develop and manage an overview of a company's legal services. General counsel should be, and many are, accountable for the cost-effectiveness of external legal services on behalf of the company's stakeholders and clients.

For this reason, the primary stakeholder for a strategic sourcing initiative should be the General Counsel (GC) or Chief Legal Officer. As an executive, the GC can mobilize the support of key board members, the CEO, the CFO and other C-suite officers. They need to be brought on board to avoid eviscerating potentially effective arrangements with law firms and other legal services providers by allowing different departments their own carve-outs and exceptions. The GC's role is to identify the range of legal stakeholders across the organization, secure their support and communicate the developments and results of the sourcing process. For these reasons, the primary stakeholders must be GCs with the support of their deputies, practice group heads, and legal operations.

WIN OVER LEGAL AS THE PRIMARY STAKEHOLDER

GCs increasingly welcome Procurement's help and support with buying legal services. However, some legal departments could be less than enthusiastic and reluctant, because the organization's executive leadership has mandated more systematic and cost-effective sourcing of all goods and services across the organization. Or the legal department may want to develop its own sourcing approach within Legal with the help of Legal Ops rather than having a sourcing program (that is imposed) from Procurement. Here, Legal is more engaged and has learned that many other organizations have successfully completed legal sourcing programs. Legal here may want to "stay ahead of the curve" rather than live with an (imposed) sourcing program.

PRACTICE TIPS:
- ☑ Procurement should prepare a formal program for sourcing legal services.
- ☑ Legal should act as the company's and Procurement's primary stakeholder.
- ☑ Procurement and Legal should be equal stakeholders in sourcing external legal services.
- ☑ Legal should be responsible for consulting and communicating with all other internal stakeholders.

To achieve sponsorship, you need to take two steps. First, organize a formal one-hour meeting that includes the Head of Procurement and a legal category specialist, the GC, a deputy and a representative from Legal Ops. Ensuring that the GC and the Head of Procurement are in attendance increases the odds of a credible commitment to a program for sourcing external legal counsel. It also lends an element of gravitas to the initial presentation and to the essential follow-up. The purpose of this meeting is to explain how Procurement can add value with a sourcing program. It should answer the question "what difference can Procurement make?"

Experienced sourcing professionals know that departments or business units, including the legal department, may prefer to manage sourcing of legal services themselves, postpone the process to another day and continue to select external counsel in traditional ways.

The success of this first meeting is measured by whether Legal declares that it wants Procurement to prepare a formal and detailed proposal describing a comprehensive sourcing program. It is not sufficient for Procurement to say that it can manage an efficient sourcing process and that it will negotiate better discounts on hourly rates through a competitive process with a limited number of legal service providers.

The second step to effectively secure sponsorship is with a second meeting where Procurement presents its formal program to Legal. It should include the following:

- A description of the qualitative and financial objectives to be achieved during the reference period (possibly over several years)
- The mandate setting out Procurement's precise role
- The detailed work plan setting out the necessary research, documentation, demand forecasts/scope of legal services, the invitations for strategic partnering/RFPs, the analysis of law firm proposals, the schedule of meetings and negotiations, and how best to measure the results
- The logistics and schedule

The sourcing program should also describe the division of labor between Procurement and the legal department for the preparation and conduct of negotiations. Legal should sign off on the program before Procurement begins the work.

CHECKLIST:

- ☑ Assess whether the legal department is likely to be an engaged or a reluctant participant and tailor your approach appropriately.
- ☑ Structure the first meeting to have the GC request a comprehensive sourcing program from Procurement.
- ☑ Structure the second meeting to present Procurement's detailed sourcing program for sign-off by the GC.
- ☑ Liaise with a member of the Legal department when preparing the program and the presentation to the legal leadership.

ROLES AND RESPONSIBILITIES

Many organizations and their legal departments are decentralized. Managers in departments or business units and in-house counsel often have their preferences for specific external legal counsel and how best to instruct them. At a minimum, they want to have a say.

It is important early on to secure agreement on the roles and responsibilities of the primary and secondary stakeholders. Ensure that the respective roles and responsibilities are properly reflected in guidelines and internal documents. Ideally, they have been vetted by the organization's internal audit function. A robust set of internal and consistent standards is required before these are communicated to the providers of the external legal services.

Make a distinction in the roles and responsibilities of each stakeholder:

- Who must be informed?
- Who must be consulted?
- Who makes the decisions?

Procurement should serve as the project manager for the legal sourcing program. The division of labor between Procurement and Legal should be detailed in the proposal and signed off before the program gets underway. The GC should designate a single representative for the program, such as the deputy GC or the most senior Legal Ops professional.

Legal should be responsible for:
- Supplying data and other reports on legal spend and on the historical use of external counsel by legal specialty, by business unit and by jurisdiction.
- Providing insight on arrangements and agreements that are currently in place with legal service providers.
- Ensuring that other stakeholders within the legal department and other departments or business units are consulted about the forecast or demand for legal services
- Ensuring that other stakeholders within the legal department and other departments or business units are consulted about their preferences for certain law firms and legal providers to be invited to participate in the sourcing process.
- Identifying a limited number of members from the legal department who will be required to read law firm proposals as well as the analysis and recommendations prepared by Procurement.
- Identifying those members from Legal who will attend meetings with the law firms. A maximum of four representatives from Legal and two from Procurement should be sufficient.

Apart from coordinating all communications with law firms and with other legal service providers during the sourcing process, Procurement should manage all of the logistics for meetings with law firms and other providers. Success and effectiveness in sourcing and negotiating legal services depends on an intimate knowledge of law firm culture, law firm economics, and the variety of relationships that an organization has with its law firms. These relationships can range from routine to specialized to highly strategic. Procurement must exhibit extensive proficiency with non-hourly fee arrangements so Legal will entrust the Legal Procurement professional with negotiating fee arrangements.

CHECKLIST:
- ☑ Secure Legal's agreement for the division of labor with Procurement before the program gets underway
- ☑ Detail the roles and responsibilities of Procurement and Legal in the sourcing program.
- ☑ Procurement should serve as the Project Manager.
- ☑ Procurement should have a deep understanding of law firm cultures and law firm economics.
- ☑ Procurement should be proficient with the full range of alternative fee arrangements.

OBJECTIVES

The legal sourcing program should have both financial as well as non-financial objectives.

Financial objectives in sourcing external counsel can be quite straightforward. Set a target to reduce the projected legal spend for the RFP reference period. It is not inevitable that legal fees should increase every year simply because law firm standard rates increase. However, the pathway to achieving significant reductions in legal expenses rarely includes greater discounts or hourly-based fee arrangements.
That approach offers marginal savings to companies that have had formal sourcing programs in place for more than ten years.

Non-financial objectives are often as important as financial ones in the drive to source external legal counsel for a formal multi-year agreement. These objectives include:

- **Reducing the number of law firms** to reduce the amount of time that the organization's in-house counsel, departments or business units spend maintaining relationships and instructing law firms. The time saved can be re-allocated to other priorities within your organization.
- **Changing the configuration of law firms** and how they work together for greater geographic coverage. Some organizations have chosen to retain a handful of firms that can coordinate local, regional and country level counsel. In effect, these firms serve as general contractors of legal services.
- **Simplifying reporting requirements**, including billing and payment protocols, to reduce the organization's administrative load for analysis and processing payments. Under the right conditions, law firms will take on this work at no cost to the organization.
- **Leveraging technology** to achieve measurable improvements in service delivery and, possibly, in legal outcomes. Efficiency and effectiveness are critical key performance indicators, but are often misaligned with non-hourly fee arrangements.
- **Changing the ratio of risk/reward** between the organization and its law firms and legal service providers through the use of alternative fee arrangements.

PRACTICE TIPS:
- ☑ List the program's non-financial objectives.
- ☑ Set a financial target for the program.
- ☑ Make sure that the qualitative and financial objectives are detailed in Procurement's proposal to Legal.

LOGISTICS, SCHEDULE, AND COMMUNICATIONS

Procurement needs to be proficient in project management to be able to achieve the work plan. This means mobilizing the human, financial, and information resources necessary to meet the plan. Procurement's program should include a detailed plan for logistics and a weekly schedule with deadlines for every stakeholder to carry out their roles and responsibilities. Weekly progress and variance reports to Legal are recommended.

Internal communications and communications with law firms and other legal services providers will consume much of your time in managing a legal sourcing program. The content of these written and in-person communications is as important as the form and process of communications with primary and secondary stakeholders. The project manager should be proficient in all forms of communication, even to the point of preparing draft communications for use by Legal in their internal consultations.

Procurement should have final accountability for the text of the RFP as well as for all of the exchanges with law firms and other providers. Include your logistics plan, the overall schedule and deadlines in your formal program for Legal.

CHECKLIST:
- ☑ The plan must include a detailed plan for logistics and deadlines.
- ☑ Procurement should report the status of the program weekly.
- ☑ Procurement should be accountable for all communications to secondary stakeholders, including law firms.

Securing sponsorship means obtaining a formal sign-off from Legal for a detailed sourcing program. Accountability for specific steps must be unambiguous. The program proposal must also pass the "SMART" test in that it must be specific, measurable, achievable with the available resources, results-oriented, and time-bound.

Procurement and Legal must regard each other as equal partners in legal sourcing. The way ahead must be clear. Accountability for specific steps must be unambiguous. Only in this way will "sponsorship" for a legal sourcing program be secured.

A WORD ABOUT LEGAL PROCUREMENT AND LEGAL OPERATIONS

Legal Procurement and Legal Ops (short for Legal Operations): When combined, these complimentary disciplines can significantly impact the dialogue between legal service providers and corporate legal teams for the benefit of your organization. To make them collaborate and get them aligned it is important to understand what each does and what benefits they can each offer your organization.

What is Legal Procurement and Legal Ops?

LEGAL PROCUREMENT

Legal Procurement applies procurement processes to the legal function through two main subsets:

Purchasing: A transaction-based function that includes the buying and selling of goods and services and the making and receiving of payments

Sourcing: The development of supply channels that represent the best value or lowest total cost and the management of suppliers via performance assessment and active collaboration

Procurement professionals use:

- Marketplace analysis
- Portfolio analysis
- Supplier preferencing
- Supply base segmentation

They also screen firms, define lower cost processes, and deliver targets

LEGAL OPERATIONS

Legal Ops is a multi-disciplinary function focused on better managing the legal department and optimizing legal services delivery within the organization

It includes:

- Litigation support & eDiscovery
- IP management
- Strategic planning
- Information/data governance & records management
- Managed services & legal process outsourcing
- Knowledge management
- Financial planning, analysis & management

Who are the professionals?

- Usually come from a **quantitative background** (e.g. finance, accounting, business)
- Are expert negotiators and vendor management professionals
- Report to the Head of Procurement and the CFO (Chief Financial Officer)

- Usually have a **legal background** (although it isn't a strict requirement)
- Undertake a wide range of operational activities
- Report to the GC (General Counsel)

What do they do?

- ✓ **Vendor management**, including RFPs
- ✓ Establish payment terms
- ✓ Negotiate contracts and manage fee proposals
- ✓ Monitor regulatory compliance and ensure compliance with agreed engagement terms
- ✓ Collect and evaluate data on services delivery by preparing decision-grade data
- ✓ Manage external spend

- ✓ Evaluate and implement technology solutions
- ✓ Optimize the management of the legal department
- ✓ Manage internal resources
- ✓ Drive internal capacity management
- ✓ Monitor internal and external costs

Who uses Legal Procurement and Legal Ops?

Companies with a **significant legal spend**

Some of the first industries to embrace Legal Procurement include pharmaceutical companies, all facets of financial services, energy companies and utilities

Companies with **large legal departments**

Organizations focused on better managing a growing number of in-house counsel and easing the GC's administrative and managerial load

What are the benefits of Legal Procurement and Legal Ops?

✓ Effective management of external legal spend and identification of opportunities for innovative cost arrangements

✓ Unbundling of legal services and matching with most appropriate providers

✓ Establishment of an efficient and robust vendor identification process

✓ Identification and management of the best value legal services and strengthening of supplier relationships

✓ More accurate costs forecasts

✓ Identification and management of technology solutions that support efficient department and matter management

✓ Creation of a repository of knowledge - e.g. contracts, precedents, and templates

✓ Identification of trends and opportunities for increased efficiencies, waste reduction and increased savings

When are Legal Procurement and Legal Ops involved?

Ideally, legal procurement is involved in the **entire process**, including the selection and ongoing management of suppliers

Legal ops manages the legal department on an **ongoing basis**

How does Legal Procurement and Legal Ops start?

▷ The CEO, CFO or Board initiates sizing legal procurement opportunities and brings in a trained buying professional

▷ Legal services were previously largely exempt from cost scrutiny but publicity about billing practices, big ticket spending and profit pressure have contributed to this shift

▷ The legal department and GC identify an opportunity for better department and resource management and set up a Legal Ops department

▷ The function has become increasingly necessary over the last decade as legal departments have increased in size

What are the potential challenges Legal Procurement and Legal Ops need to overcome?

- In-house counsel may fear potential loss of power and influence if new processes are introduced

- Concerns about a business and process driven approach disrupting long-standing provider relationships

- In-house counsel reluctance to separate legal practice from delivery management

- Lack of resources to support the function

- Lack of collaboration between in-house counsel and Legal Operations

MEET STAKEHOLDERS' EXPECTATIONS

A successful sourcing program actively engages stakeholders at key intervals. Effective stakeholder engagement ensures that you meet their expectations and instills a sense of accountability for the outcome.

To meet stakeholder expectations, align your overall strategy to that of your stakeholders. You must fully understand your legal department's priorities (both procurement and non-procurement related) to formulate your strategy, priorities, and objectives. Conflicting objectives will lead to frustration, lack of buy-in, reputational damage for Procurement and, most importantly, non-delivery.

Every stakeholder will have or develop their own view as to what they consider the best outcome. It is important that you distinguish between what stakeholders want and what the organization expects to be delivered. Communicate the project deliverables up-front to level-set expectations and to remain within the scope of the project both from a time and content perspective.

Stakeholder engagement needs to start well before any specific project commences. You need to establish and maintain a trusted relationship on an ongoing basis as it is integral to the success of your projects for when problems arise.

In a first step, identify your stakeholders. It is likely that your list of potential stakeholders will be larger than you might assume at first. Your stakeholders' level of involvement will also vary: Your organization's legal department is likely made up of different teams focusing on specific areas such as human resources, mergers and acquisitions activity, data protection, intellectual property and others. In addition, the finance department may also be interested in the review given that any savings present an opportunity to reduce budgets. The compliance department is keen to ensure that governance requirements are met, and the risk team is concerned about any impacts on risk to the business.

Ask these key questions:
- ☑ How much influence does each stakeholder have?
- ☑ Are the stakeholders interested in the project? Should they be interested?
- ☑ What do you need from the respective stakeholder?
- ☑ What is your existing relationship with the respective stakeholder?
- ☑ How will the stakeholders react to potential change?

Once you have identified the key stakeholders, you understand the impact that they could potentially have on your project. Conduct a simple stakeholder mapping using the Power/Interest model.

MATRIX STAKEHOLDER ANALYSIS
ADAPTATION OF MENDELOW'S POWER-INTEREST GRID

NOTE: The example is for illustrative purposes only. Populating this grid can help identify and prioritize stakeholder involvement. Remember that every review will be different, and that you will need to tailor your approach depending on the circumstances.

The legal sourcing strategy project's sponsor (typically the GC) needs to set expectations for the project to kick off initial communication. (This is not the role of Procurement.) Your GC should communicate their expectations including roles and responsibilities as well as the rationale behind the project.

Keep in mind that not every (potential) stakeholder will welcome being part of your new sourcing strategy, especially when you expect them to be actively involved. Some of your (potential) stakeholders may consider the project unnecessary, overly complicated, and/or time consuming. For that reason, the GC should acknowledge stakeholders' concerns, even if these cannot be addressed or solved. This is particularly important for the key players you identified in your stakeholder mapping. They ultimately determine how successful this project will be and should therefore be actively involved in the review.

Structure your projects with realistic goals and timeframes with the scope and roles and responsibilities clearly defined. Consider implementing a framework (similar to the one below) that provides clear structure, communication channels and escalation processes. Schedule regular meetings and make sure that every meeting is fully minuted, highlighting agreed action points, risks and issues and shared with the stakeholders. Clear action plans and tracking against these will ensure that everyone is aware of progress against key deliverables, whether timelines are being met and whether there are any roadblocks to overcome. Update project documents and make them readily accessible to all those involved.

Example of structuring a project:

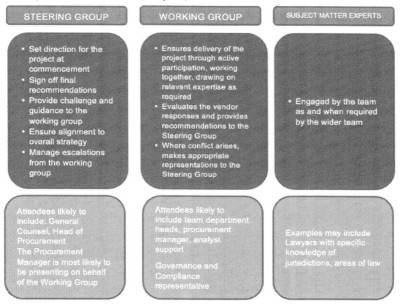

After the initial kick-off meeting, gather key stakeholder members to:

☑ Sense check their understanding of the project's objectives

☑ Re-enforce expectations of the project sponsor

☑ Obtain a common understanding of the roles and responsibilities of those involved

☑ Establish a sense of team identity

☑ Identify any issues that need to be addressed

☑ Agree how the team will engage (e.g. weekly calls, face-to-face meetings etc.)

☑ Determine how project updates will be recorded

☑ Align on a clear escalation process for issues not resolved or where an agreement cannot be reached

The project should be governed by a robust project scope and terms of reference document that all key stakeholders had input into. Developing this document is time well spent. Keep it updated to ensure that deliverables remain relevant and are addressed, but also in order to avoid scope creep.

PRACTICE TIPS:
- ☑ To manage your stakeholders' expectations, communicate clearly and operate a culture of no surprises.
- ☑ Have a clear discussion and escalation process to ensure that everyone is aware of the current status, progress against deliverables, and next steps.
- ☑ An effective communication strategy should be discussed and agreed with the stakeholders.

A simple project scope and terms of reference document may look like this:

Stakeholder	Engagement Level	Proposed Communication Strategy	Frequency
Head of HR Legal	Key player to the review	Engage in working group 1:1 discussions re business requirements	Weekly calls Ad-hoc
Finance Manager	Needs to be kept informed	Share project reports	Monthly
Data Protection Team Lawyers	Needs to be kept informed	Engage them in the business requirements to be gathered for the specific area Delegate updates to Data Protection Team Head	Ad-hoc as per plan At key milestones

PROJECT SCOPE AND TERMS OF REFERENCE DOCUMENT

Keep other stakeholders that are not actively engaged in the day-to-day work of the project updated and satisfied. Formulate an appropriate communication strategy to do so. Depending on their importance, take into account their preferred style and ensure that you remain as user-friendly as possible.

CHECKLIST:
- ☑ Develop and nurture an ongoing relationship with regular dialogue outside of specific sourcing activities
- ☑ Ensure that your stakeholders fully understand the role of Legal Procurement for the project
- ☑ Align legal department and Legal Procurement strategy
- ☑ Identify the ultimate decision maker(s) and ensure that they are fully engaged or have empowered their delegates
- ☑ Undertake a stakeholder identification and prioritization exercise
- ☑ Engage stakeholders and instill a sense of accountability
- ☑ Develop a framework which allows for communication, discussion, and escalation
- ☑ Document stakeholder engagement requirements

SCOPE LEGAL SERVICES

Scoping is a critical part of sourcing legal services externally. It should be part of your RFP designed to inform potential providers of the scope of work (SOW) to help achieve your organization's objectives. You can scope work for individual matters, multiple matters, or a collection of matters over time. In this context, scoping refers to multiple matters or a collection of matters over time.

PRACTICE TIPS:
- ☑ Set measurable financial and non-financial objectives when scoping legal services.
- ☑ Ensure that the RFP sets out the non-financial objectives.
- ☑ Align the scope of work with the financial objectives of the RFP.

HISTORICAL DATA

Scoping legal services for sourcing purposes means describing each category of work, the types of matters and the complexity mix for each category, and the estimated volumes of work by category and by jurisdiction. The scope of work should set out the optimal practice patterns – for example by staffing ratios – by legal category.

Not every organization wishes to reveal this level of detail, perhaps reticent that by doing so you will raise expectations in firms or providers that you cannot fulfill. However, all estimates are provisional, and none constitutes a guarantee of work to any firm. The advantages of sharing this information outweigh the perceived risk of doing so because firms will be more prepared to accept the organization's non-financial and financial objectives when preparing proposals and negotiating favorable long-term arrangements.

The past is not a predictor of the future when it comes to expressing the demand for legal services. However, historical data should be your place to start. A matter management system is a better source of data than data from your accounting system. Still, companies that maintain a matter management system may find that some legal activity is not captured because it is a pass-through charged to customers, to insurers, to special projects or because it is cost-shared with other companies in the same industry. Matter management systems will generate basic spending data, hours, and categories of legal work.

In addition, consider asking the law firms or legal service providers in your database (or those providers that were paid more than a minimum threshold in the last two years, e.g. $10,000), to produce data in a uniform format to generate a more comprehensive picture of the organization's historical demand for legal services.

A basic spreadsheet supported by clear definitions of each legal category is sufficient to secure what you need from firms and other providers. Make sure that the spreadsheet covers at least two complete calendar (or financial) years plus as many months as possible in the current year.

You need data for each legal specialty. It should be broken down by jurisdiction or region, by legal specialty and matter complexity, and with the total hours per year for each. The annual hours should be available by experience level for lawyers and technical staff to map practice patterns and staffing ratios for each law firm and legal specialty.

In the example below, there were 20 litigation matters worked on for a total of 965 hours. The firm regarded only one matter to be routine, ten to have mid-level complexity, and nine were deemed complex. The client might consider the mix to be less complex than the firm's reporting suggests. The data also shows that 38.8 percent of the hours were worked by lawyers with 15+ years of experience and 30.3 percent were worked by entry level associates (with 0 to 3 years of experience). Knowledge of the twenty matters in question and comparison with staffing patterns from previous years and from other firms could suggest that the scope of work in an RFP might stipulate an optimal staffing ratio for litigation.

CHECKLIST:
- ☑ Source at least two years of data from matter management systems.
- ☑ Issue a Request for Information (RFI) to each law firm or provider that billed a minimum threshold in one of the last two years.
- ☑ Use uniform category definitions and provide your firms and providers with these and a spreadsheet to supply data for at least five variables.
- ☑ Ensure that the data covers all external legal activity regardless of where the expense is charged.

Overall Totals

Complexity Level	Total Fees	# of Matters	15+ Yrs	8-14 Yrs	4-7 Yrs	0-3 yrs	Paralegal	Other	Total Hrs	Rate
			Hours by experience level							
Routine Matter	$ 256 149.00	132	100.5	41.6	4.3	94.6	22.2	635.6	898.8	$ 284.99
Mid-level Matter	$ 404 194.50	34	181.4	261.5	133.2	231.5	128.1	115.2	1 050.9	$ 384.64
Unique/Complex Matter	$ 2 464 468.75	30	1 648.7	1 215.4	452.8	1 615.5	158.0	436.4	5 526.8	$ 445.92
Overall Totals	$ 3 124 812.25	196	1 930.6	1 518.5	590.3	1 941.6	308.3	1 187.2	7 476.4	$ 417.96
			25.8%	20.3%	7.9%	26.0%	4.1%	15.9%		

Primary Category: BCI Hospitality

Complexity Level	Total Fees	# of Matters	15+ Yrs	8-14 Yrs	4-7 Yrs	0-3 yrs	Paralegal	Other	Total Hrs	Rate
Routine Matter	$ 39 596.00	51	34.9	1.2	0.1	0.5	13.8	102.4	152.9	$ 258.97
Mid-level Matter	$ 60 114.00	4	34.0	46.2	24.8	32.7	-	23.3	161.0	$ 373.38
Unique/Complex Matter	$ 198 841.00	3	51.3	130.3	-	328.8	10.7	149.5	670.6	$ 296.51
Overall Totals	$ 298 551.00	58	120.2	177.7	24.9	362.0	24.5	275.2	984.5	$ 303.25
			12.2%	18.0%	2.5%	36.8%	2.5%	28.0%		

Primary Category: Corporate Law

Complexity Level	Total Fees	# of Matters	15+ Yrs	8-14 Yrs	4-7 Yrs	0-3 yrs	Paralegal	Other	Total Hrs	Rate
Routine Matter	$ 158 082.00	75	31.6	29.1	1.2	20.8	6.4	527.7	616.8	$ 256.29
Mid-level Matter	$ 90 952.00	2	25.1	75.4	3.0	7.2	54.5	22.9	188.1	$ 483.53
Unique/Complex Matter	$ -	-	-	-	-	-	-	-	-	$ -
Overall Totals	$ 249 034.00	77	56.7	104.5	4.2	28.0	60.9	550.6	804.9	$ 309.40
			7.0%	13.0%	0.5%	3.5%	7.6%	68.4%		

Primary Category: Formation of Scottish Airline

Complexity Level	Total Fees	# of Matters	15+ Yrs	8-14 Yrs	4-7 Yrs	0-3 yrs	Paralegal	Other	Total Hrs	Rate
Routine Matter	$ 14 440.00	1	6.9	2.3	-	23.3	1.4	5.5	39.4	$ 366.50
Mid-level Matter	$ 30 044.00	2	16.6	31.3	1.0	3.8	0.8	13.2	66.7	$ 450.43
Unique/Complex Matter	$ -	-	-	-	-	-	-	-	-	$ -
Overall Totals	$ 44 484.00	3	23.5	33.6	1.0	27.1	2.2	18.7	106.1	$ 419.26
			22.1%	31.7%	0.9%	25.5%	2.1%	17.6%		

Primary Category: General Commercial Matters

Complexity Level	Total Fees	# of Matters	15+ Yrs	8-14 Yrs	4-7 Yrs	0-3 yrs	Paralegal	Other	Total Hrs	Rate
Routine Matter	$ 8 694.00	2	7.0	6.9	-	1.0	-	-	14.9	$ 583.49
Mid-level Matter	$ 55 533.00	5	23.5	22.4	-	58.6	32.3	32.3	169.1	$ 328.40
Unique/Complex Matter	$ 194 554.00	6	156.1	41.0	6.8	152.5	4.6	39.7	400.7	$ 485.54
Overall Totals	$ 258 781.00	13	186.6	70.3	6.8	212.1	36.9	72.0	584.7	$ 442.59
			31.9%	12.0%	1.2%	36.3%	6.3%	12.3%		

Primary Category: Litigation and Dispute Resolution

Complexity Level	Total Fees	# of Matters	15+ Yrs	8-14 Yrs	4-7 Yrs	0-3 yrs	Paralegal	Other	Total Hrs	Rate
Routine Matter	$ 1 618.00	1	1.0	1.6	3.0	-	0.6	-	6.2	$ 260.97
Mid-level Matter	$ 40 134.50	10	-	46.5	87.6	8.8	31.7	3.0	177.6	$ 226.05
Unique/Complex Matter	$ 364 329.75	9	105.6	326.7	201.6	40.8	99.2	7.5	781.4	$ 466.28
Overall Totals	$ 406 082.25	20	106.6	374.8	292.2	49.6	131.5	10.5	965.1	$ 420.77
			11.0%	38.8%	30.3%	5.1%	13.6%	1.1%		

Primary Category: Regulatory Affairs

Complexity Level	Total Fees	# of Matters	15+ Yrs	8-14 Yrs	4-7 Yrs	0-3 yrs	Paralegal	Other	Total Hrs	Rate
Routine Matter	$ 15 851.00	1	5.1	-	-	24.7	-	-	29.8	$ 531.91
Mid-level Matter	$ 11 572.00	2	2.6	-	2.2	18.4	-	-	23.2	$ 498.79
Unique/Complex Matter	$ 42 630.00	1	19.9	55.1	-	1.0	0.2	31.9	108.1	$ 394.36
Overall Totals	$ 70 053.00	4	27.6	55.1	2.2	44.1	0.2	31.9	161.1	$ 434.84
			17.1%	34.2%	1.4%	27.4%	0.1%	19.8%		

Primary Category: Tax Law - Compliance

Complexity Level	Total Fees	# of Matters	15+ Yrs	8-14 Yrs	4-7 Yrs	0-3 yrs	Paralegal	Other	Total Hrs	Rate
Routine Matter	$ 16 848.00	1	12.8	0.5	-	24.3	-	-	37.6	$ 448.09
Mid-level Matter	$ -	-	-	-	-	-	-	-	-	$ -
Unique/Complex Matter	$ -	-	-	-	-	-	-	-	-	$ -
Overall Totals	$ 16 848.00	1	12.8	0.5	-	24.3	-	-	37.6	$ 448.09
			34.0%	1.3%	0.0%	64.6%	0.0%	0.0%		

Primary Category: Tax Law - Transaction Structuring (domestic and international)

Complexity Level	Total Fees	# of Matters	15+ Yrs	8-14 Yrs	4-7 Yrs	0-3 yrs	Paralegal	Other	Total Hrs	Rate
Routine Matter	$ 1 020.00	-	1.2	-	-	-	-	-	1.2	$ 850.00
Mid-level Matter	$ 115 845.00	9	79.6	39.7	14.6	102.0	8.8	20.5	265.2	$ 436.82
Unique/Complex Matter	$ 1 664 114.00	11	1 315.8	662.3	244.4	1 092.4	43.3	207.8	3 566.0	$ 466.66
Overall Totals	$ 1 780 979.00	20	1 396.6	702.0	259.0	1 194.4	52.1	228.3	3 832.4	$ 464.72
			36.4%	18.3%	6.8%	31.2%	1.4%	6.0%		

SAMPLE DATA SHEET

Provided the data that you sourced internally and from your law firms is comprehensive, then it should be straightforward to determine the volume of activity (hours and number of matters), total fees and effective rate, as well as the staffing patterns for each legal specialty for each law firm or provider by jurisdiction, and for the organization and its subsidiaries for each year covered by the RFI.

As part of a supporting document, your law firms and providers should describe discount and favorable fee arrangements that were applied to the spreadsheet data. For organizations that retain a large number of primary and secondary firms and providers across multiple jurisdictions, asking the firms and providers to provide pricing information is more efficient than sourcing fee arrangements internally. Apart from rates, internal data may not be current or well-documented.

Procurement should prepare the analysis of the RFI data and discount arrangements and discuss these with the legal department. Few organizations are aware of the extent and detail of their external legal activity, including:

- The precise number of primary and secondary firms and providers used across the organization each year.
- Fees paid to each firm or provider by jurisdiction and legal specialty (not including disbursements and taxes).
- The number of matters and hours for each firm or provider, by specialty and jurisdiction.
- Variations in effective rates, discount arrangements, and alternative fee arrangements for similar work.
- Variations in practice patterns and staffing ratios by law firm or provider for similar work.

A comprehensive review and discussion with the Legal department should generate clearer objectives for the RFP including:

- The preferred number of primary and secondary firms and providers for the future.
- Preferred practice patterns and staffing ratios by legal specialty.
- Opportunities for non-hourly fee arrangements and for more favorable financial terms.
- How best to formalize and improve internal protocols and operating practices governing how legal work is assigned and how it is managed with law firms and other legal services providers.
- How the legal department and law firms and other legal services providers can introduce and manage detailed matter budgets for all files over a minimum threshold (e.g. 50 hours).

To prepare or approve a detailed matter budget and to monitor variances requires substantive legal knowledge and project management skills that cover:

- Phases and tasks taken from the relevant legal code set
- Planning assumptions for each phase and for each task
- Probability for each assumption
- Allocation of partner, associate and paralegal hours for each task
- Protocols for variance reporting and change orders as the matter progresses
- Linking the matter plan and budget to hourly and non-hourly fee arrangements

PRACTICE TIPS:
- ☑ Reduce the number of primary and secondary firms to create significant critical mass for the remaining firms.
- ☑ Set targets to reduce the effective rate by legal specialty.
- ☑ Establish optimal practice patterns by legal specialty.
- ☑ Introduce rigorous operating practices and matter budgeting to reduce hours worked.

FORECAST DEMAND

Some organizations hesitate at divulging projected volumes or hours of work for each legal specialty and jurisdiction in their RFP, concerned that doing so could be interpreted as a guarantee or commitment. For this reason, it is a common practice for the procurement process to be limited to creating a panel of qualified firms with the best possible hourly discount. However, this approach fails to leverage data to stimulate non-hourly pricing, innovation, and efficiency from the law firms selected. It also fails to support many non-financial objectives. In short, your organization is not using its buying power to maximum advantage.

Developing a clear SOW for purposes of the RFP should be a joint process between Procurement and Legal. Consider a SOW that covers at least three years. Express the demand for each specialty and jurisdiction as the total hours per year. Adjust projections up or down from historical patterns, based on the legal department's knowledge of work that is recurrent and work such as litigation, regulatory matters, and transactions which tend to be more irregular. Volumes can vary for each calendar year. The text of the RFP should explain the complexion and configuration of the legal work in the SOW.

It is leading practice to migrate significant volumes of work to non-hourly pricing (so called alternative fee arrangements or AFAs) to stimulate efficiency and to mitigate the number of hours used by a firm. The introduction of rigorous matter budgeting for files exceeding the defined threshold will also reduce the number of hours used. Experience shows that organizations have been successful in reducing the SOW (hours) by up to 15 percent with the combined use of AFAs and legal matter budgets.

One of the most important ways to reduce the cost of external legal services is by rethinking and prescribing staffing ratios and practice patterns in law firms. Law firms often under-delegate tasks to less senior (and less costly) lawyers and paralegal staff. Partners carry out tasks that could be assigned to qualified associates. Unmanaged practice patterns add at least ten percent to the effective rate, and therefore to the overall cost of a matter. Analysis of the law firm data and benchmarking leading staffing practices should convince Procurement and the legal department to prescribe optimal staffing ratios for each legal specialty.

For example, the SOW for 10,000 hours of litigation work per year in a given jurisdiction could include staffing ratios of 15 percent for senior partners, 20 percent for junior partners, 40 percent for senior associates, 10 percent for junior associates and 15 percent for paralegals.

Keep in mind that the ratio for the portfolio of matters will vary by type of litigation and jurisdiction. The above example is for illustrative purposes.

PRACTICE TIPS:
- ☑ Include the volume of hours (even if on a provisional basis) in the SOW.
- ☑ Factor in the effects of rigorous matter budgeting on demand for external counsel.
- ☑ Express the SOW by region and jurisdiction, legal specialty and complexity mix.
- ☑ Detail the SOW using optimal staffing ratios for each category of work.

There are important strategic and practical considerations when preparing the SOW for the RFP, such as changing the number and configuration of primary firms. Creating a critical mass of work for each firm that is sustainable over the RFP reference period means reducing the number of firms invited for proposals. A reduced number of law firms also helps maximizing negotiating leverage. Consider that 10,000 hours per year represents a full workload for only 5.5 lawyers and paralegals. Experience suggests that typically 95 percent of legal work at all levels of complexity can be done by panel firms.

A three-year projection in the SOW is an estimate at best. There will be fluctuations in volume by jurisdiction and specialty from year to year. Favorable fee arrangements, even hourly arrangements, will be influenced by the amount of work your law firms and other providers hope to receive. The RFP should state that the terms of engagement with each primary law firm or provider will contain an annual review and adjustment mechanism which is both retrospective and prospective. Such reviews will consider variations from the anticipated scope of work and the potential for adjustments to fee arrangements.

Most law firms and other legal services providers today have extensive experience with formal sourcing initiatives. Leading practice suggests that legacy work should be included in the SOW for the RFP, even if the same firms continue the work. Legacy firms usually accept legal matter budgeting and optimal staffing ratios as part of a concerted cost management program.

The composition of law firm panels changes for many reasons. Lead partners leave the firm or Legal changes its preferences, and because some legacy firms emerge from the sourcing process as comparatively too expensive. The SOW for the first year following a multi-year sourcing process should allow for a transitional period to the new panel configuration.

Comprehensive scoping of work when sourcing legal services should reflect both financial and non-financial objectives. Obtain historical data about legal activity and about financial arrangements from your matter management systems and from law firms directly. Prepare a forecast of the demand for external legal services containing hours and levels of matter complexity for each legal specialty by region or jurisdiction.

RFPs should seek to reduce panel sizes, prescribe optimal staffing ratios by specialty, and target a reduction from current pricing. Once sourcing is complete, incorporate an annual review and adjustment mechanism. Allow for the work of legacy firms and provide for a transitional process when changing the configuration of firms or introducing new pricing arrangements.

CHECKLIST:
- ☑ Create a critical mass SOW with fewer primary and secondary firms in mind.
- ☑ Ensure that an annual review and adjustment mechanism for the SOW is detailed in the RFP for multi-year arrangements.
- ☑ Include the work of legacy firms in the SOW.
- ☑ Anticipate transitional provisions for the post-sourcing period.

IDENTIFY THE RIGHT FIRMS AND PROVIDERS AND SOLICIT PROPOSALS

IDENTIFY THE RIGHT FIRMS AND PROVIDERS

Finding the right firms and providers requires a clear understanding of what you actually want them to do. You need a clearly articulated and agreed legal category strategy that sets out:

- The type(s) of legal advice required for the duration of the appointment
- Jurisdictional coverage needed
- How many providers you have now, doing what, and would like going forward
- How work will be allocated between providers
- Whether (and under what circumstances) providers will be working with internal legal teams or independently
- Historical spend analysis
- Pricing targets (including any cost saving requirements)
- Strategy for incumbent providers (e.g. can they be replaced or do they need to be retained because of experience/ongoing matters/cost of change/shared technology investment)
- Business or leadership preferences with reasoning for firm retention/moving away

The first step in finding the right candidates for your legal RFP is to understand what they are likely to be doing for you and where, even if only at a high level.

If your business is acquisitional, you might need mergers and acquisition advice. If you do a lot of property transactions, you will need someone with that expertise. If you are about to embark on an employee restructuring program, you may need employment advice. Are you going to be undertaking 'bet the business' transactions or more commoditized work? You may not have the exact timescales or volume requirements, but your business strategy should give some clues as to your likely future needs.

Historical spend data is also useful in helping choose candidates. As we mentioned before, past work is no indication of future needs, but there is a 'business as usual' contingent to external legal support that recurs annually. In the absence of any clear future direction, historical is better than no information (especially for the bidders).

SHORTLIST REQUIREMENTS

Having analyzed historical spend data and decided on what types of advice you are likely to need going forwards, you go on to research the marketplace in order to start creating a shortlist of possible candidates for your RFP.

The most fundamental decision in creating your candidate shortlist is how many firms you want to work with. If you have multi-practice area, multi-jurisdictional needs and want a sole supplier, or a professional support lawyer panel, your shortlist will look very different to that for a single jurisdiction, limited work-type panel.

Other considerations include:

- **Representation**: Whether you want physical representation in (a) specific location(s) or would be happy for work to be undertaken from anywhere. Are you ok with working with a firm's 'best-friend network' in jurisdictions where they do not have a presence or does that rule them out?
- **Type of Provider**: The type of legal provider you want to work with and why. Do you need Tier 1 law firms because your business needs, risks, and stakeholders are best served by them or is your external work more commoditized and best undertaken by regional providers? Can an alternative legal services provider (ALSP) undertake your work instead of a traditional law firm? Do you need Counsel or Company Secretarial services in addition?
- **Organizational preferences and relationships** that need to be maintained: Many candidates for RFPs are chosen because of existing relationships or business/legal leadership preferences, even if Procurement's research shows that this particular firm is not the best fit in terms of coverage or cost targets.
- **Commercial considerations**: The commercial requirements from any RFP process should help dictate your shortlist. If you are looking to reduce external spend, consider strategies such as reducing the number of providers, changing the location or types of firms from which services are provided or moving to a single supplier relationship.
- **Governance requirements**: Some providers are better than others in terms of fulfilling reporting and governance needs. Being clear about your expectations will help candidates to assess whether they are able to work with you efficiently.

- **Technology requirements and strategy**: Experience and roadmaps for working with specific technologies such as contract automation tools, electronic discovery (term used mostly in the U.S.)/electronic disclosure (term used mostly in the UK) (short: eDiscovery/eDisclosure) platforms, electronic billing systems and other legal tech may influence your shortlist.
- **How easy is a firm to work with?** Consider this a key determinant in whether an incumbent firm should make it to your candidate shortlists. Consider the following:
  - Price credibility – historical & current
  - Accuracy of estimates and budget management
  - Ability to create and demonstrate cost and process efficiencies
  - Delivery of service improvements and innovations
  - Proactive relationship management
  - Active matter tracking and accurate matter intake

ESTABLISH THE CANDIDATE LIST

Armed with your shortlist requirements, you can now establish a candidate list through a combination of internal discussion and review, discussion with providers and market analysis.

Internal Shortlist Evaluation: Your internal discussions should focus on areas such as:
- Which incumbent firms and providers need to be on the shortlist list? Why?
- Do any incumbent firms and providers need to be retained regardless of the RFP process? If so, should they be going through a different process (subject to governance/legal considerations being met)?

- Do any new firms or providers need to be included based on stakeholder preferences? If so, which?
- Would non-traditional legal services providers (ALSPs/LPOs/consultancies etc.) be an option?
- Which commercial or legal conditions need to be fulfilled by a candidate (e.g. turnover, insurance levels, minimum team sizes, approach to ongoing claims against the provider, ability to operate in specific jurisdictions, etc.)?

PLEASE NOTE: It is not good practice to ask providers to participate in your RFP because they are incumbents but no longer appear to have the right profile for your (new) needs. Just because they have historically been a good fit does not mean they will be going forward, whether that be from a service or cost perspective. Being really clear about the likelihood of a candidate winning work from you will help them to make a measured commercial decision as to whether participation is worth their investment.

Discussion with Potential Candidates: Beware of your attractiveness as a client. All clients are not equal to firms and providers. In fact, some clients are actually quite unattractive to law firms based on their commercial behaviors and/or value-add requirements. As clients, you might forget that law firms and other legal providers are also evaluating you:
- How attractive you are to work with
- Whether your engagement and matter management processes will drive cost into their provision
- Your historical and likely fee management behaviors (e.g. do you continually expect additional discounts and fee write-offs?)
- Whether they can meet your legal and governance needs and still make a decent profit
- How commercially fair and open you are

Discussing with incumbents and potential new providers what they are looking for in a client will help you figure out whether they are a good fit, and help them evaluate whether they want to work with you. Be honest with yourself as to whether you are a good match, and given them the opportunity to say 'no thanks, no hard feelings'.

Market Analysis: There are different approaches to market analysis to find the right candidates for tender:
- Engaging cost and or service benchmarking via an external agency or by a consultant
- Asking Procurement contacts and forums for recommendations
- Undertaking market research (e.g. via legal publications to find out who other organizations in your sector or industry are using for their external legal services)
- Reviewing legal provider websites for specialism and jurisdictional cover
- Asking incumbent providers for recommendations (e.g. for partnerships)
- RFI (Request for Information) processes

Using an RFI Process to Find Candidates: Running an RFI process can be an expensive undertaking for both the tenderer and prospective candidates. It should only be used when there is either a governance need (e.g. in some public sector procurement), or when you cannot reach a shortlist using any of the steps outlined.

A good RFI should clearly articulate the business problem you are seeking to solve by appointing an external legal provider, for example:
- Providing additional capacity/capability
- Rationalizing legal provision
- Achieving cost-reductions

- Introducing cost-competition
- Appointment of a legal panel
- Meeting changing business needs
- Outline of any wider tender process and where the RFI fits within that.
- The likely scope of services (work-type, jurisdictional requirements, transaction volumes)
- Any engagement model preferences or requirements (e.g. legal panel, preferred supplier list, sole-supply arrangement)
- Expected number of candidates to be taken forward into any additional tender stage and likely appointment duration
- Historical legal spend profile
- Guidance on the required format of the response
- The evaluation process and timescales for the RFI

PRACTICAL TIP: Beware that no-one wants to invest time in responding to a tender that they are never going to win, or in reading something that does not really stand a chance. Be clear with potential candidates about your requirements and provide as much data as possible to help ensure relevant responses. The more information you give to potential candidates at the RFI stage, the greater the chances of identifying the right candidates for your needs.

Depending on your organization's culture, the right "cultural fit" may be one of your critical non-financial objectives when identifying the right candidates. Organizations are recognizing customers' and stakeholders' growing awareness of societal issues such as diversity and inclusion as well as sustainability and social impact. Increasingly, public pressure, and in some parts of the world, regulatory requirements now hold organizations responsible not just for their own business practices but also those of their service providers.

Organizations' choices and behavior have significant influence on their firms and providers. If social impact and sustainability/diversity and inclusion are important aspects for your organization, you will want to work with firms and providers that are aligned with your values. Through specific RFP questions and closer assessment of firms' programs, you are able to assess whether your firms' or providers' social impact and sustainability/diversity and inclusion programs are a core and strategic element of their organization or only token gestures and "check-the-box" exercises.

When you select providers, of course you first need to ensure that their skills and expertise match those you need for a given matter or project. Once that threshold is met, however, you can confirm whether your organization is partnering with firms and providers who share your values and commitments and whose behaviors are consistent with your own organization's social objectives.

How to assess law firms and other legal services providers*: Ask questions about the firm's or provider's social impact and sustainability/diversity and inclusion program.*

- ☑ *You can do this in the RFP document and you should most certainly do so in the finalists' presentations. Do the answers match the descriptions on their website? A red flag would be if the partners in the finalist presentations do not know anything about the firm's social impact and sustainability/diversity and inclusion program.*

☑ *Peruse the firm's website to understand where they position social impact and sustainability/diversity and inclusion. Is it only listed in the Careers section of the website? If so, that may indicate that the firm does not have a holistic program. It conveys that they know their program is important to recruits, but that the firm does not really see it as core to their business nor core to who they are.*

☑ *Research who the firm is partnering with in their social impact and sustainability/diversity and inclusion programs. (See the list of external frameworks below.) Are they "committing random acts of kindness" that reflect partners' pet projects? Or do they clearly state their desired impact with respect to certain issues and partner with other organizations to achieve greater impact? Again, this is very telling with respect to whether social impact and sustainability/diversity and inclusion are part of the business or simply a "side committee" pursuing random projects.*

Communicate your expectations of meaningful social impact and sustainability/diversity and inclusion programs to your firms and providers. Several frameworks, tools, and service providers are available to help ensure these programs are meaningful.

☑ *Review the firm's or provider's website for a discussion of its social impact and sustainability/diversity and inclusion efforts.*

☑ *Compare the RFP responses to social impact and sustainability/diversity and inclusion questions with the discussions on the firm's or provider's website.*

☑ *Question the lawyers in the finalist presentation. Do they know about, understand, and embrace the firm's/provider's objectives when it comes to social impact and sustainability/diversity and inclusion?*

☑ *Is the firm or provider aligning its social impact and sustainability/diversity and inclusion program with any external frameworks?*

☑ *Is the firm or provider partnering with third-party organizations to achieve greater impact?*

☑ *Is the firm or provider certified?*

☑ *How well aligned are the firm's or provider's objectives and areas of focus with your organization's social impact and sustainability/diversity and inclusion goals?*

☑ *Did the firm or provider propose any collaboration opportunities with your organization for greater progress on mutual social impact and sustainability/diversity and inclusion goals?*

RESOURCES FOR SOCIAL IMPACT AND SUSTAINABILITY

A growing number of frameworks are emerging that make it easier to assess and evaluate the sincerity and robustness of your firms' and providers' social impact and sustainability programs. Check if your firms and providers have aligned their programs to any of these frameworks, indicating a more outward and collaborative focus. Here are several of the most important frameworks:

United Nations Global Compact (UNGC) is the world's largest corporate sustainability initiative and a call to companies to align strategies and operations with universal principles on human rights, labor, environment, and anti-corruption. It also takes action to advance social goals. Companies can join the UNGC by becoming either a signatory organization or a participatory organization. www.unglobalcompact.org

United Nations Sustainable Development Goals (UNSDGs) address the global challenges we face, including poverty, inequality, climate change, environmental degradation, peace, and justice. The 17 Goals are all interconnected and intended to be achieved by 2030. Many companies align their social impact and sustainability programs to help make progress toward the UNSDGs.
www.un.org/sustainabledevelopment/sustainable-development-goals

Certified B Corporations have met rigorous standards of social and environmental performance, accountability, and transparency. A growing global community of certified B Corporations across industries work together to redefine success in business so that one day all companies will compete not just to be the best in the world but also to be the best for the world. www.bcorporation.net

Global Reporting Initiative (GRI) helps businesses and governments worldwide understand and communicate their impact on critical sustainability issues such as climate change, human rights, governance, and social wellbeing. This enables real action to create social, environmental, and economic benefits for everyone. www.globalreporting.org

International Organization for Standardization (ISO) 26000 provides guidance to those who identify respect for society and environment as a critical success factor. Application of ISO 26000 is increasingly viewed as a way of assessing an organization's commitment to sustainability and its overall performance.
www.iso.org/iso-26000-social-responsibility.html

You can also work with a third-party assessment or audit company to help analyze the behaviors and social impact of your firms and providers. These assessment tools help verify the actual impact of your firms' and providers' programs and behaviors:

American Legal Industry Sustainability Standard (ALISS) is an online self-assessment tool that measures law firm's environmental sustainability. It allows law firms to take stock of their efforts to promote energy efficiency, conservation of energy and resources, recycling, and related measures. ALISS is intended to provide guidance that helps firms identify opportunities to enhance their sustainability programs and practices (www.lfsnetwork.org).

Other non-legal specific assessments companies include **EcoVadis** (www.ecovadis.com) and **IntegrityNext** (www.integritynext.com).

SAMPLE RFP QUESTIONS
FOR SOCIAL IMPACT AND SUSTAINABILITY

- ☑ *Please share the environmental policy statement your organization has in place for your supply chain.*
- ☑ *Do you have a Sustainability Policy for corporate social responsibility (CSR) that covers environmental, social and governance (ESG) issues? If so, please provide a copy.*
- ☑ *Do you have a Sustainability Code for your suppliers/subcontractors/service providers?*
- ☑ *Please provide the name and contact details of the individual responsible for implementing the Sustainability Program at your firm*
- ☑ *Does your organization:*
  - o *Have processes in place to address ESG impacts in your supply chain?*
  - o *Integrate ESG principles in your purchasing decisions?*
  - o *Purchase environmentally-preferable services and products?*
  - o *Partner with suppliers who are committed to ESG principles?*
  - o *Partner with suppliers who measure and publicly report environmental performance and goals?*
- ☑ *Does your organization have a Supplier Diversity program?*
- ☑ *Are you able to provide your organization's supplier diversity metrics?*
- ☑ *Do you currently have sales, service, or distribution channels in place with women, veteran, and/or minority owned businesses?*
- ☑ *What percentage of your organization's total contracting and procurement spend for the prior year was with women, veteran, service disabled veteran, and minority-owned businesses?*

☑ *Does your organization track first and second tier diversity spend with a proper tracking tool?*

☑ *Does your organization identify diverse suppliers for second-tier opportunities?*

☑ *Is your organization willing to provide quarterly second tier spend report outlining expenditures with certified diverse suppliers under our contract?*

RESOURCES FOR DIVERSITY AND INCLUSION

Resources for identifying diverse-owned law firms and other legal services providers include:

The National Association of Minority & Women Owned Law Firms (NAMWOLF): The trade association for minority and women owned law firms. www.namwolf.org

NMSDC (National Minority Supplier Development Council) certifies minority business enterprises. www.nmsdc.org

WBENC (Women's Business Enterprise National Council) certifies women-owned businesses in the U.S. www.wbenc.org

WEConnect International certifies women-owned businesses outside the U.S. www.weconnectinternational.org

Women-Owned Law (WOL): A trade group to advocate for and empower women entrepreneurs to revolutionize the business of law. www.womenownedlaw.org

NGLCC – The National LGBT Chamber of Commerce certifies LGBT enterprises. The NGLCC also hosts the National Legal Industry Council (NLIC) to promote supplier diversity efforts within the legal profession. www.nglcc.org/Legalindustry

Disability:IN is a network of corporations intended to expand opportunities for people with disabilities. www.disabilityin.org

NVBDC (National Veterans Business Development Council) certifies veteran-owned businesses. www.nvbdc.org

Further resources for diversity and inclusion in the legal industry:

Diversity Lab/Mansfield Rule
Mansfield Rule is a volunteer program where law firms signed up to meet commitments regarding making changes to their firm staffing practices in an effort to make improvements in diversity and inclusion. www.diversitylab.com/

American Bar Association Model Diversity Survey
https://www.americanbar.org/groups/diversity/DiversityCommission/model-diversity-survey/

American Lawyer, Diversity Scorecard
https://www.law.com/americanlawyer/2020/05/26/the-2020-diversity-scorecard-rankings-and-demographic-leaders/

Chambers Diversity and Inclusion Leaders
https://diversity.chambers.com/event/chambers-diversity-inclusion-awards-north-america-2020/

Minority Corporate Counsel Association (MCCA) & Vault Database
https://www.mcca.com/resources/reports/2020-vault-mcca-law-firm-diversity-survey/

SAMPLE RFP QUESTIONS
FOR DIVERSITY AND INCLUSION

- ☑ *Are you Mansfield Rule certified or in the process of participation?*
- ☑ *Do you have a Chief Diversity Officer or other leadership-level position for diversity?*
- ☑ *Do you have a Diversity Committee or similar team driving diversity change at the firm?*
- ☑ *Are partner and firm leader populations (CFO, CIO, HR Lead) at least [30] percent diverse?*
- ☑ *Does your new recruit, associate pool or other staff make-up include diverse candidates [30-40 percent]?*
- ☑ *Do you have diverse candidate recruiting, retention and mentorship programs?*
- ☑ *Does your website include a dedicated page sharing details of its diversity practices?*
- ☑ *Are involved in community activities or collaborating with industry trade groups that are actively promoting and sponsoring diversity and inclusion initiatives?*
- ☑ *Do you have formal processes or practices in place for Supplier Diversity with regards to goods and services they purchase to conduct business (i.e. indirect or direct purchase, such as offices supplies, consulting, computer hardware or software, printing, marketing services, meetings and events, etc.)?*
- ☑ *Are you a diverse-owned and/or certified diverse-owned business entity?*

SUPPLIER DIVERSITY

You may also want to include supplier diversity. Supplier Diversity is defined as a proactive business program that encourages the use of minority-owned, women-owned, veteran-owned, LGBTQ+-owned, service disabled-veteran owned, historically underutilized business, and Small Business Administration-defined small business.

For U.S.-based corporations with government contracts, doing business with diverse-owned vendors is a requirement, but usually grows into a business advantage. There are reporting and auditing processes to support supplier diversity tracking for both, the government and non-government initiatives. Many procurement departments have formal Supplier Diversity positions on staff to manage such programs, inclusive of trade organization relationships, event sponsorship and attendance, report management, new supplier vetting, supplier networking, coaching and any other procurement processes that have an impact supplier diversity goals, objectives and outcomes. Supplier Diversity can apply to all areas of spend across indirect and direct spend towers.

HOW TO ASSESS A FIRM'S/PROVIDER'S DIVERSITY & INCLUSION APTITUDE

If you want to employ formal initiatives related to diversity within a law firm or legal services provider program, consider the following key elements for evaluation:

(1) Diversity at firm level
- *Overall firm staffing*
- *Firm diversity initiatives (commitments, programs, etc.*

(2) Diversity at legal matter/case/project level

(3) Supplier Diversity
- *Engagement of 51+ percent diverse-owned firms or legal services provider*
- *Supplier Diversity: firms/providers engaged have an inclusive procurement process where diverse-owned law firms and other legal services providers are invited to bids or RFPs for the purchase of goods or services; also known as second tier supplier diversity)*

In addition to the SAMPLE RFP QUESTIONS FOR DIVERSITY AND INCLUSION listed above for your law firms and legal services providers in a general RFP, you can include specific questions when appropriate in matter or project-level RFPs. The goal is to request/require your firms and suppliers to provide a diverse team of people to work on your assignments:

SAMPLE RFP QUESTIONS
TO ASSESS YOUR FIRM'S/PROVIDER'S ABILITY
TO PROVIDE A DIVERSE TEAM

Identify a diverse staffing goal or metric for your law firm/provider program and provide details in the RFP questionnaire. Ask specific questions on the firm or provider's ability to meet this criterion (consider a Yes/No question with space for comments). Review the firm's website to understand their overall position on diversity and inclusion and assess if the RFP response matches the firm's/provider's diversity and inclusion culture.

- ☑ *Is your firm/company willing to provide a diverse team of people, assigned to this project, that matches our requirement of [x] percent women, minority, LGBTQ+, veteran, disabled or other diverse team members? Yes/No answer required.*
- ☑ *If your firm/company cannot meet this requirement at the start of work, please explain why and what action you will take to remedy this.*
- ☑ *Please share information about any firm/company initiatives that will directly impact staffing on matters where clients are requiring diverse teams to be assigned.*

REQUESTS FOR PROPOSAL

Requests for proposal (RFP) or tenders are now regularly used to select law firms, other legal service providers and legal tech providers. Law firms today are used to filling in RFPs, even if your in-house legal department might suggest otherwise.

The key to a successful RFP for legal services lies in:
- Understanding and communicating the objectives of the RFP activity
- Designing a process that is proportionate with the expected outcomes
- Having a clearly defined set of expected outcomes and measurement processes aligned to the RFP's objectives
- Providing enough spend and volume data for firms and providers to create value-based pricing proposals
- Clear RFP governance and communication

RFPs can be very challenging for those trying to respond. You risk getting generic responses that make selection difficult unless you provide clear objectives for your RFP process. Provide either detailed historical or predicted spend data or at a minimum, scope of work.

Be clear about the objectives of your RFP both internally and externally with your legal services providers. This allows you to design a cost-effective process that delivers the expected benefits. It also allows your providers make an informed decision as to whether they are able to meet those objectives, your objectives are aligned with their own strategy, and they want to invest time and effort to participate in your RFP.

Be transparent about why you are running the RFP process and how your objectives align with your legal category strategy and the organization's overall strategy. Typical RFP objectives are:

- Achieving cost savings
- Supplier rationalization
- Cost benchmarking
- Securing sector, work-type and/or jurisdictional cover (e.g. linked to corporate expansion)
- Securing or standardization of value-added activities
- Introducing or adhering to spend governance requirements
- Improving legal operations management
- Meeting legal requirements (e.g. in public procurement)
- Introduction of legal technology and/or project management expertise
- Introducing cost competition for a specific matter or group of transactions

THE RFP PROCESS

Conducting an RFP process is expensive for both your organization as well as those you invite to win your business. Scoping, designing the RFP, responding, evaluating, debriefing are all resource-intensive activities and law firms and legal services providers often see the processes as disproportionate to the potential prize they can gain.

Design your RFP processes with your desired outcome in mind. If you are generally happy with your external legal providers but want to reduce overall spend, you could discuss this with your law firms and providers and implement a spend management program rather than using an RFP. Could you negotiate different terms with them or give up some of the value adds?

Not having to provide additional services may give you rate reductions that meet your RFP objectives, without the expense of going through the RFP process.

Your stakeholders in the legal department as well as some of your firms and other legal services providers may not be fully aware of the difference between RFx or tender methodologies. Be very clear to bidders about why you are using a particular process and what it entails. Use the below overview with your legal stakeholders and providers to ensure their understanding:

Pre-Qualification Questionnaire (PQQ): Buyers looking for a provider for a particular contract need to evaluate the potential firms and providers on particular criteria. A PQQ often kick-starts the procurement progress, even in the absence of full tender documents, for the PQQ to be launched, Procurement only needs information about the project or panel, as well as the assessment criteria that would be used to identify the right providers.

Invitation to tender (ITT): Also known as a call for bids – is a formal, structured procedure for generating competing offers from different potential providers in supply or service contracts, often from companies who have been previously assessed for suitability by means of a supplier questionnaire or pre-qualification questionnaire (PQQ).

Request for information (RFI): Is a market enquiry issued to one or more prospective providers. Its purpose is to research, gather information about the category, the provider's solutions, capacity and/or capability, historical spend for the organization, and key market intelligence.

It is typically used when an organization lacks full understanding of the product or service needed and/or of the category, and wishes to increase that understanding prior to seeking commercial offers through a Request for Quotation (RFQ) or RFP. RFIs are usually part of a multi-stage procurement process, with the next step involving shortlisting potential respondents based on the RFI replies and inviting commercial offers.

Request for quotation (RFQ): Is a market enquiry issued to prospective providers, typically for lower value or simple goods/services. It requests providers to submit qualifications or specialized expertise in response to the parameters and scope of services required. Its purpose is to invite commercial offers from a number of providers to secure competition, and gather information about the provider's solutions, their lead time, service support, cost/price, and other dimensions of their value proposition.

Request for tender (RFT): Is a market enquiry issued to prospective providers for higher value and/or more complex solutions. Its purpose is to invite commercial offers from a number of providers to secure competition and to gather information about the provider's solutions, capability, cost/price, and key market intelligence. The evaluation of the RFT may require the buyer to compare qualitative aspects of the provider's value proposition, such as quality and service, with quantitative aspects such as price.

Request for Proposal (RFP): Is a market enquiry issued to prospective providers for higher value and/or more complex solutions. Its purpose is to invite commercial offers from a number of providers to secure competition, and to gather information about the provider's solutions and capability, cost/price, and key market intelligence. RFPs are commonly used for legal services and legal technology solutions.

If you do need to issue an RFP, design the process to be as straightforward as possible and appropriate – in terms of effort – for the likely legal spend and any savings targets you have in mind. Be clear about why you chose a particular methodology and whether this is the first of several steps (e.g. PQQ & ITT) or the entire process.

Consider whether you need the standard tender steps of:
- Written proposals
- Q&A sessions
- Presentations
- References
- Electronic auctions (eAuctions)
- Negotiations

In fact, challenge yourself whether each of these steps is necessary and consider the costs involved in each step. If your objective is cost savings, a drawn-out process may cost you more than you can save.

Allocate an appropriate timescale for each part of the RFP process that allows for quality responses from your bidders. Issuing an RFP on the Friday before a holiday and expecting your answers to be returned on Monday or Tuesday the following week is not likely to endear you to anyone, calls into question your attractiveness as a client and will likely result in a sub-standard response.

Consider whether you need slightly different processes and questions for incumbent and potential new providers. For example, it is very challenging for a new provider to convincingly describe how they will effectively work with you when compared to an incumbent who knows your organization well. Consider whether you may need more detailed initial briefings, extra Q&A sessions, or less specific questions for new bidders?

Consider sharing your evaluation criteria and weightings with your bidders as it will help focus their responses. For example, if your main objective is cost savings, you may want to be clear about that or if you would not consider any providers without presence in a specific jurisdiction. You will get better responses as a result. Progressive companies typically share many, but not all, of their non-financial and financial objectives in the RFP and in the meetings with law firms and other legal services providers.

Be clear about the type of services and relationship you are looking for. For example, communicate whether you are looking for a panel (and if so, how big you intend your panel to be?), a sole provider, occasional help or anything else. Be clear about the length of the appointment, and issue terms and conditions with the RFP documents. This information will help your bidders decide whether this opportunity is for them.

Design your RFP questions carefully and be clear to your bidders about what you are looking for in the response. The current trend for case studies is useful for teasing out experience, but be clear about what you want them to show, for example ways of working, direct sector experience, commercial outcomes. Be really specific in what you are looking for.

SAMPLE QUESTIONS YOU MAY WANT TO ASK

- "We are interested in your ideas on the topics of cost reduction, transparency, and efficiency."
- "Please describe your approach to process improvement and project management."
- "We ask you to illustrate how your firm ensures the desired outcome for our matters while guaranteeing the most efficient use of our resources."

94

- "How do you measure your performance against our business requirements?"
- "Our company uses process improvement methodologies such as Six Sigma and Lean. We expect our providers to use equally efficient techniques. Please explain your firm's methodologies."

Avoid the "tell us anything else we might find useful" question. It is a red flag to bidders that perhaps you do not really know what you want.

DEFINE RFP OUTCOMES

Clearly define the outcomes you expect from the RFP and explain to your law firms and other legal services providers how you will evaluate bids relative to the outcomes. Also inform them about your ongoing, post-selection performance measurement processes. This is critical for both internal stakeholder management throughout and after the RFP process, and for ongoing performance and relationship management.

Typical RFP outcomes include:
- Achieve [x] percent cost savings targets
- Appointment of a legal panel or reduction in panel size
- Appointment of a sole supply arrangement
- Legal function outsourcing (in whole or part)
- Increase/decrease scope and jurisdictional coverage for externally sourced legal services
- Secure additional depth/breadth of legal expertise to support business objectives or current matters

Consider explaining how you will evaluate participants against each outcome and the relative importance of different criteria. Some Procurement professionals provide bidders with weighted critical success factors or evaluation criteria as this helps the bidder understand where to focus their efforts in the RFP response and tailor their offering to meet your needs. Again, if the required outcome of your RFP is cost savings above all else, then be clear about that. It allows participants to choose whether the opportunity is for them this time and will improve your likelihood of getting quality responses that meet your needs.

Additionally, be clear about ongoing post-RFP performance measurement processes. This allows your bidders to evaluate whether they can meet your requirements and whether it is worth their investment. For example, participating in an extensive RFP process with detailed regular reporting requirements may not be attractive if fees are unlikely to exceed $[x-thousand] per year.

VOLUME DATA

Unless you provide your law firms and other legal services providers with some indicative historical data of likely volume, you are unlikely to get the best possible pricing. Not providing this critical information, particularly in panel selection processes, is akin to asking a builder to quote on a kitchen extension without giving any specifications. You would not expect them to give you a meaningful quote under those circumstances, or would you?

Providing data on possible fee revenue helps bidders set rates and fees. They will need to recover cost associated with your service delivery and client management. Without indicative spend data, their estimate will be bigger due to the larger risk they will calculate into your proposal.

PRACTICE TIPS:

If you are concerned that:

- Your historical spend is not necessarily indicative of your future needs: Experience shows that any data is typically better than none. External support needs usually do not change dramatically year over year for many areas. Please note that this is generally not true for transactions and regulatory work, such as antitrust.
- You only have patchy or poor data: Be upfront about it. This is helpful to bidders as it enables them to understand your spend management challenges and they can suggest monitoring and governance processes that can help improve data capture.

RFP GOVERNANCE AND COMMUNICATION

An effective RFP requires clearly defined governance that is appropriately robust and proportionate to your process. Set realistic timelines that take into account how long it takes to evaluate and score responses as well as the availability of key personnel and decision makers. Plan your governance process well, agree to with your stakeholders, and document it. Poor governance not only has cost implications in managing the RFP process, but can also reflect poorly on your organization's ability to manage your operations, negatively affecting pricing. Your RFP governance should involve a multi-disciplinary team including Procurement and Legal as primary stakeholders and Legal Ops, Finance, Business lines, and Risk as secondary stakeholders.

CHECKLIST for RFP governance:

- ☑ Appoint a core evaluation team with clearly defined roles and responsibilities.
- ☑ Create a detailed RFP plan that is signed off by all key stakeholders.
- ☑ Develop a scoring methodology that is aligned with critical success factors and selection criteria as well as a scoring process.
- ☑ Get agreement on a communications plan that unmistakably outlines processes (such as managing questions related to the RFP) and expectations regarding the management of 'business as usual' communication by incumbents throughout the RFP process
- ☑ Communicate a detailed RFP plan to all your bidders, taking into account work events (e.g. year-end) or holidays that might affect availability of key resources.
- ☑ Communicate your communications plan to all bidders.

UNDERSTAND PRICING OF LEGAL SERVICES

To achieve significant reductions in legal expenses set formal financial targets as part of written pricing plans agreed with Legal. Complete this as part of securing sponsorship and long before drafting an RFP. Experience shows that greater discounts on hourly-based fee arrangements only offer marginal savings. The RFP should describe both non-financial objectives as well as the scope of work to be aligned with the financial objectives of the RFP, even if the targets are not formally revealed to law firms.

The best price for a portfolio of legal work depends on a combination of factors, including:
- A multi-year forecast of the demand that reflect estimates, not guarantees, of work volumes
- The fewest possible number of firms (convergence)
- Agreement on staffing/delegation distributions for each portfolio and category of work
- A commitment to rigorous matter budgeting by phase/task and by timekeeper

PRICING SPECIFICATIONS

Managing the expectations of all stakeholders, including law firms and other providers, requires considerable preparation when it comes to pricing. This is essential when it is the objective to prioritize AFAs and to make these the predominant rather than the occasional method of pricing legal work. Procurement needs to have a robust understanding of law firm economics and the related profitability variables, of law firm cultures, and of law firm compensation systems for partners and associates for the firms that the organization uses.

PRACTICAL TIPS:

- ☑ Prioritize the use of non-hourly, "alternative" fee arrangements (AFAs) in the RFP as the dominant form of pricing.
- ☑ Ensure that Procurement, Legal Ops, and the legal department have a common understanding and a mastery of advanced AFA practices.
- ☑ Set firm pricing targets and align these with the terms of the RFP.

Setting the Stage: Preferably as a preamble in your RFP, articulate the organization's principles and objectives. For example, the organization wishes to:

- ☑ Secure the best value in legal services through a careful balance of expertise, service delivery and cost.
- ☑ Enter into a limited number of partnering agreements for legal services with a small number of primary service providers and a handful of supplementary regional firms or subject-matter focused providers.
- ☑ Be among the most innovative of organizations when collaborating with law firms and other legal services providers.
- ☑ Streamline the administration of partnering arrangements for the organization, its law firms, and other legal services providers.
- ☑ Promote continuity and efficiency in the use of legal resources.
- ☑ Secure predictability in the costs of legal services, within a forecasted volume of legal services.

Consider asking each firms the following pricing-related statements and questions as part of the RFP.

"The firm is asked to bill either an agreed fixed fee, a flat fee, a performance fee, or a variation of an hourly rate. The preferred arrangements for the reference period are to be finalized during our discussions with you in the coming weeks. You will not have the option to a bill higher price if this would exceed the agreed pricing arrangements for the reference period, except if approved by us on a matter-by-matter basis.

The firm is encouraged to propose innovative methods to mitigate costs. This can include teams with more members based in less expensive markets where your firm has offices or where you have arrangements with correspondent firms. We will not compromise unique legal expertise. However, we are actively seeking less costly arrangements from you as a partnering firm.

- *What is your pricing philosophy for the next three or four years?*
- *What would be your preferred partnering and pricing arrangements with us for the type of work and the period covered by this RFP?*
- *How do you support the rigorous use of project/case budgeting and management tools for all files over a certain threshold, e.g. 50 hours, including for complex and strategic matters?*
- *Has your firm introduced legal project management software and training for partners in the last two years?*
- *Describe the resources and practices used to source matter budget precedents in your firm.*

- *Describe the technology your firm could apply in support of cost-effective collaboration and reporting of activity for our organization.*
- *Do you currently have the resources available to provide the services for which you are bidding?"*

Experience shows that unmanaged practice patterns in law firms add at least 10 percent to the effective rate. The RFP should prescribe "optimal staffing distributions" for categories and portfolios of work. Ask firms to propose compact and stable teams of senior and junior professionals as well as paralegals to cover the reference period. Law firm responses to the RFP should state the extent of their support and the related conditions for the application of the organization's optimal staffing distributions in pricing legal work.

PRACTICE TIPS:
- Incorporate a statement of principles and objectives into the RFP ensuring that several call for innovation in pricing and service delivery.
- Build in enough specific questions dealing with legal costs and pricing to allow a comparative evaluation of law firm proposals.
- Remember that prescribing optimal staffing distributions for each category and portfolio of legal work reduces the cost of legal services by at least 10 percent.

CHOOSE THE MOST EFFECTIVE FEE ARRANGEMENT

There are three basic types of fee arrangements: Hourly fees, fixed and flat fees, and contingency/percentage-based fees, plus hybrids and variations for each of them. For instance, a fixed fee can be combined with a performance fee tied to a result. Hourly billing is still often the default fee arrangement since hourly rates require a minimum amount of change to operating practices by the organization and by the law firm. However, this is not the same as cost-effective pricing. Designing an alternative fee arrangement that is effective and appropriate for a category of matters, possibly for hundreds of matters with a broad range complexity levels covering a three to five-year reference period, requires a credible demand forecast and a critical mass of work.

Switching to AFAs requires your law firms to focus on your organization's priorities. Make it clear that the choice of pricing should:

- ☑ Stimulate **efficiency** in legal work, enough to reduce the hours needed to support a portfolio of matters by at least ten percent over time.
- ☑ Reward the **effectiveness** of legal work, as measured by the expected results.
- ☑ Promote **innovation** initiatives that pass the SMART test and which improve efficiency and/or effectiveness.

COMPARE FEE ARRANGEMENTS

A cross-section of arrangements follows beginning with a variation on hourly rates.

Blended Hourly Rates: Individual hourly rates can and should be replaced with a blended hourly rate for each category of legal work. A properly configured blended rate should:
- Reflect agreed staffing distributions for a matter or a group of matters to encourage the delegation of tasks within law firm teams
- Include annual adjustments for experience
- Include inflation so the blend is not increased during the reference period
- Build in all volume discounts
- Result in a reduction of 10 percent in the effective rate when compared to discounted individual rates

Keep in mind that a blended rate has almost no effect on law firm efficiency, that is to say on the number of hours worked by the law firm. Matter budgets and AFAs are better suited to managing efficiency.

Fixed and Flat Fees: Fixed and Flat Fees are fee arrangements that provide you with such predictability. A fixed fee for a portfolio of work should stimulate the organization and the law firm to rely on leading practices for matter budgeting, project management and work allocation.

Fixed fees can be calculated for a portfolio of work (e.g. 3,000 hours of litigation per year for three years) by building on a negotiated blended rate. A fixed monthly fee can be set for 36 months even though volumes may fluctuate from month to month.

Should the annual variance on the estimated work volume should be more or less than ten percent, you need to have review and adjustment mechanism.

Flat fees differ from fixed fees and are most often applied to high volume, regular work in specializations such as real estate, insurance, intellectual property, collections, corporate secretarial activity, and some aspects of labor law among others. Flat fee schedules can be converted to fixed fees provided a critical mass of work can be assembled across a multi-year period. Doing so provides additional leverage in price negotiations with law firms.

Fees for Performance and Innovation: Performance-based fees are retrospective fees based on KPIs. They establish performance indicators in the RFP and in the terms of engagement with each firm. Performance indicators typically include results, service levels, efficiency, and cost predictability. Some organizations have migrated to a more advanced, yet simpler, form of performance fee with their primary firms because they have been satisfied with service levels, results, and cost management over the years. In such cases, performance can be more developmental in nature and can take the form of an Innovation Fee that supplements a fixed base fee. Reserve 10 to 15 percent of the overall legal budget to fund innovation.

Include joint research and development initiatives that benefit your organization in the short term. Propose a specific budget for each project. Upon completion, each project should be evaluated under the guidance of the legal department. The extent of success determines how much of the project budget is paid to the firm.

PRACTICE TIPS:

- ☑ Decide on the combination of blended hourly rates, fixed and flat fees, and performance-based fees for each category and portfolio of work in the RFP.
- ☑ Only use blended rates as a building block to arrive at a base fee target for each category and portfolio of work.
- ☑ Reserve at least ten percent of the legal budget to recognize performance as measured by results, service levels, efficiency, and cost control. Alternatively, the same budget can be dedicated to innovation that is focused on effectiveness/results.
- ☑ Describe the hybrid pricing plan in the RFP and ask law firms to commit – at least in principle – to this type of AFA.

REVIEW PROPOSALS AT STANDARD AND DISCOUNTED FEES

Evaluate RFPs on the following non-financial criteria:

- ☑ Commerciality and familiarity with your organization's industry and your organization's primary customers
- ☑ Coverage and expertise for each region and/or specialty
- ☑ Client relationship and account management
- ☑ Project management, knowledge management, and process improvement
- ☑ Staffing distributions and collaboration across a network of offices and local firms
- ☑ Technology to improve the cost-effectiveness of legal services

Score each proposal on each of the above criteria (0 points for 'Does not meet', 1 point for 'Meets expectations' and 2 points for 'Exceeds expectations').

Twelve points represent a perfect score. Eliminate firms that do not meet expectations for commerciality and familiarity, coverage and expertise as well as staffing/collaboration before you evaluate the financial portion of the proposals.

PRELIMINARY FINANCIAL EVALUATION

Compare the proposed cost of legal services for each category and portfolio of legal work for each firm before starting of price negotiations. See the below example for a multi-regional litigation portfolio with 3,000 hours per year. Firms are listed from most to least expensive after the discount is applied. For comparison purposes, the table assumes that a firm is allocated 100 percent of the work.

Law firm	Average Rate	Discounted Rate	12-month cost
Law Firm D	$494.50	$432.69	$1,298,063
Law Firm L	$543.17	$398.55	$1,195,650
Law Firm A	$594.33	$386.32	$1,158,950
Law firm G	$464.53	$378.59	$1,135,784
Law Firm H	$523.48	$355.97	$1,067,902
Law Firm B	$492.00	$344.40	$1,033,200
Law Firm K	$396.60	$282.00	$846,002
Law Firm E	$350.93	$279.49	$838,474
Law Firm C	$355.97	$275.41	$826,233
Law Firm J	$304.92	$243.94	$731,810
Law Firm F	$327.49	$ 243.80	$ 731 400

PRACTICE TIPS:
- ☑ Conduct a rigorous non-financial evaluation of each proposal with a view to eliminate some firms.
- ☑ Prepare a comparison of each firm's standard and discounted prices for each category and portfolio of work for each region, with a view to eliminating some firms before commencing fee negotiations.

COSTING A PRELIMINARY ALLOCATION TO LAW FIRMS

Organizations have been reducing or converging the number of law firms on which they rely on for decades. Convergence is a sourcing strategy that creates a larger share of work for the successful firms. This in turn provides your organization with more leverage in price negotiations. In the context of multi-year agreements or multi-national coverage, the law firm has access to a critical mass or work and to a dependable, but not guaranteed, revenue stream.

An organization with progressive management practices should be able to commit, but not guarantee, a volume of work for several years in exchange for a fixed price. The organization secures budget predictability and firms have regular cash flow. Provided annual volumes are sufficient, collar arrangements, ranging from ten to 15 percent are usually sufficient for a firm to secure predictable cash flow and to stimulate efficiency in the law firm. The preliminary evaluation of Firm K's cost (see Table above) is $864,002 for 3,000 hours per year. A three-year cost at $282.00 per hour for 9,000 hours is $2,538,006 or $70,500 per month. A ten percent collar on the fixed price means that the monthly payments will not change unless the worked hours are less than 8,100 or more than 9,900 over the three-year reference period.

Fixed fees for a portfolio of work can easily evolve into hybrid fees consisting of a fixed base amount plus a variable portion tied to key performance indicators.

Setting aside transitional arrangements with legacy firms which are not retained after a new procurement cycle, the organization should prepare a preliminary work allocation of 100 percent of the RFP's SOW to the smallest number of firms. See the example for a portfolio of 25,000 hours per year covering employment, labor, benefits advice, affirmative action, and strategic advice regarding Human Resources with requirements in 15 jurisdictions.

Area of law	Firm A Low Cost	Firm B Coverage	Firm C Coverage	Firm D Strategic Relationship and Specialized
Affirmative Action (4,000 hours)	4,000 hours @ $325 $1,300,000			
Benefits Advice (4,000 hours)				4,000 hours @ $425 $1,700,000
Employment Law (10,000 hours)		5,000 hours @ $360 $1,800,000	5,000 hours @ $340 $1,700,000	
Labor Law (3,000 hours)		1,500 hours @ $380 $570,000	1,500 hours @ $360 $540,000	
Strategic Advice (4,000 hours)				4,000 hours @ $675 $2,700,000
Totals	$1,300,000 4,000 hours @ $325.00/hr	$2,370,000 6,500 hours @ $364,62/hr	$2,240,000 6,500 hours @ $344.62/hr	$4,400,000 8,000 hours @ $550/hr

Preparing a first draft of the costing allows the legal department to consider the best balance of cost, coverage, and competence/expertise. Additional drafts for different allocations will affect the applicable discounts and the overall cost.

Prepare a preliminary costing before the second (or final) round of price negotiations. In the example above, Firm D would be paid $4,400,000 per year for 8,000 hours. The three-year price would be $13,200,000 for 24,000 hours of Benefits and Strategic Advice. The fee would not vary if the hours worked (assuming a ten percent collar) range from 21,600 to 26,400 over the three years.

PRACTICE TIPS:
☑ Procurement should agree with the legal department on the type of relationship that the organization wants with its primary and secondary law firms. This is essential before finalizing pricing.
☑ Aim for a fixed fee with a collar, plus a variable fee for performance/innovation with each of your primary firms.
☑ Prepare variations of work allocation and costing after the first round of fee negotiations. Continue doing so until allocations and negotiations are completed.

FINAL EVALUATION

Carry out a final comparison of prices after completing a second round of price negotiations with the successful firms and after making the final/provisional allocation of work. Eliminate firms:

☑ Based on the results of the non-financial evaluation.
☑ After a comparative evaluation of prices, but before negotiations.
☑ After a first round of fee negotiations.
☑ After a last round of price negotiations and a final/provisional allocation of the portfolio of work.

Discount thresholds are likely to be annual. Law firms often express them as annual fees. Conduct a diligent review at 6-month and 12-month intervals to determine the extent of convergence to fewer firms as well as the efficiency of file transfers from legacy firms. Firms with hourly or blended hourly pricing will report and bill activity monthly. Firms with a fixed fee arrangement for a portfolio should report activity levels quarterly even if payment is in equal monthly amounts. Conduct a formal retrospective and prospective analysis of activity levels and work allocation practices annually.

It is common to adjust the base fee at the end of twelve months when activity levels are significantly outside the range you anticipated at the outset of the agreement and if they are likely to continue as a trend after the first year. The annual review is also an opportunity to compare the geographic distribution and the complexity mix of matters with the RFP's scope of work and your organization's planning assumptions for each firm's work allocation.

When it is likely that the initial estimates for work volume will materialize after the first year, it might be more practical to pay the additional hours worked beyond the collar (at the agreed blended rate) or to be refunded (at the agreed blended rate) for hours paid but not worked that are below the collar (i.e. below the 90 percent mark). Another option is to roll these variances into subsequent years rather than "true up" on an annual basis.

PRACTICE TIPS:

- ☑ Conduct a retrospective and prospective analysis of activity levels, file complexity and geographic distribution of work for all firms each year.
- ☑ Reset the base fee for fixed fee firms after year 1 when the multi-year trend warrants.
- ☑ Evaluate each law firm annually (formalized and in writing). Share the results with each firm regardless of the pricing arrangements in place. Poor performance could influence payments to or refunds from non-hourly firms.

ASSESS AND NEGOTIATE WITH FIRMS AND PROVIDERS

ASSESS FIRMS AND PROVIDERS

The outside counsel selection process can be a demanding endeavor, requiring a lot of time, preparation, and maintenance. Even once you conducted your RFP, reviewing and assessing each response to select firms that every stakeholder can agree on is a challenging task. But we are not trying to discourage you. On the contrary! Use a formal scoring system to simplify the selection. This warrants a formal and structured process because the success of an RFP hinges on accurate assessment of how well every solicited proposal meets the needs set forth by your stakeholders.

While preparing a formal scoring system requires organization and careful planning, the benefits of using scorecards as part of outside counsel selection substantially compensates for the additional work upfront. Scoring provides formal tracking of the outside counsel selection process. It also provides a complete picture of each candidate outside counsel firm in one place and presents the relevant information in an easily accessible format.

The process of quantifying the selection criteria itself, and scoring the firms accordingly, leads to a more accurate and impartial assessment compared to a fully subjective final firm ranking achieved without thorough review of the breakdown and individual sub-score assignment. Scoring allows you to compare law firms and other legal services providers along the same or similar dimensions and to place additional emphasis on the metrics that are most critical to your legal department and other stakeholders involved, such as results and cost-effectiveness.

Ultimately, the process provides rankings of the candidate firms and providers that are supported by quantitative data and can appropriately withstand challenges to the RFP outcome by the participating firms and internal or external stakeholders.

Without a formal quantitative methodology of scoring and ranking candidate firms, subjectivity inevitably governs the selection process and comparisons between firms are inconsistent and arbitrary. Subjectivity and individual preference will guide the selection, and individual biases and preferences of stakeholders will play the primary role. This is especially true in the face of multiple proposals with varying pros and cons across different dimensions with no effective way to organize or analyze the data. Without a system in place, it becomes much easier to fall back on the "tried and true" firms that have always been used. This also excludes your organization from new partnership opportunities that could potentially create value and save costs, subverting the very purpose of conducting the RFP in the first place.

Without scoring, comparisons between law firms and other legal services providers are also less precise. There is no easy way to directly compare the strengths and weaknesses of different firms for a given criteria. Similarly, it is challenging to approximate how you should evaluate different firms' and providers' strengths in meeting a certain criterion given that the criteria themselves vary in importance to the legal department and other stakeholders. Scoring does not completely eliminate issues of inconsistent or arbitrary evaluation, but the process of creating score ranges and assigning relative weights beforehand will reduce impartiality and increases the reliability of the resulting decision.

Formal scoring allows you to standardize the process of evaluating RFP responses. You assign different quantitative values to firms according to their respective abilities to meet the pre-determined evaluation criteria. You can use the resulting scores to compare different law firms and legal services providers against the legal department's (and other stakeholders') needs as well as against the other candidates. The goal is to select the law firm or service provider that offers the best fit.

Scoring in the Legal Procurement context can vary by the rigor required to meet a department need. A less rigorous scoring system may take into account only a couple of categories on which stakeholders are interested in assessing different firms. A moderate option may consider five to seven different categories, and a more intense option may consider eight or more different categories of evaluation criteria. Choose the appropriate type of scoring depending on the importance of selection and the utility of the increased documentation and granularity that comes with more data. Naturally, your choice will also depend on the time and resources that you have available for implementing the scoring system.

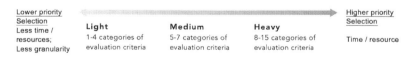

| Lower priority Selection | | | | Higher priority Selection |
| Less time / resources; Less granularity | **Light** 1-4 categories of evaluation criteria | **Medium** 5-7 categories of evaluation criteria | **Heavy** 8-15 categories of evaluation criteria | Time / resource |

TYPES OF SCORING

While the complexity of the scoring process may vary depending on the priority of the RFP, the basic steps can be adapted to suit your legal department's needs:

Step 1: Form an evaluation committee

Consider using multiple scorers to increase objectivity and department-wide consensus. When choosing the proposal evaluators, consider stakeholders who understand department needs and the requirements of the specific matter or project. Involve those who are already invested in the RFP process. Consider who else should be on the core team of evaluators and who are subject matter experts who may be helpful in evaluating specific parts of the proposals.

Step 2: Identify key selection criteria

The selection criteria for scoring should match those established for the original RFP that served as the basis for the proposals. Consider both capability standards and cost standards:

- **Capability standards** may include factors such as historical performance, lawyer/team expertise and experience in similar matters, and staffing and geographic coverage (bench strength and depth).
- **Cost standards** are typically driven by Legal Procurement and may include factors such as (hourly) rate, pricing models/fee arrangement, historical total cost, and concessions (e.g. travel discounts). Also consider tailoring to specific areas of legal service such as corporate, intellectual property (IP), procurement, and employment.

Do not forget to include the following criteria: quality, value, client focus, and alignment of values (between provider and your organization).

Step 3: Develop a scoring methodology

Start by sorting your evaluation criteria in different categories: By topics, by needs vs. wants, and by priorities (high, medium, low, nice to have). Use categories to help organize the evaluation process, especially if there are evaluators who are only scoring some, but not all criteria.

Next, assign relative numerical weights to each criterion based on priority sorting.

Finally, determine a scoring scale to assign raw scores for each criterion. The score ranges may vary depending on the possible participant responses. Choose simple numeric ranges that offer only as much granularity as required to capture the spread of possible responses. For example, yes/no responses could be designated 0-1, while 1 to 5 or 1 to 10 ranges could better capture other responses with more options.

Step 4: Create a scorecard

Create a simple and clear scorecard that every evaluator will use. The scorecard can be a worksheet that contains a raw score entry for each criterion, its relative weight based on its pre-determined priority, and space for any additional comments. The scorecard should also make clear what the selection criteria entail. The following sample scorecard may be adapted to the level of complexity that a given RFP requires.

Candidate Firm/Provider:				Evaluator:
Selection Criteria (give definitions/ examples to ensure consistent scoring)	RFP Section(s)	Weight	Raw Score (1-5)	Comments
1. Quality	Quality	50%		
2. Value	Value	20%		
3. Client Focus	Client Focus	10%		
4. Alignment	Alignment	10%		
5. Diversity	Diversity	10%		
Summary Score:	Weighted Average (sum of raw scores multiplied by weights)			

SAMPLE SCORECARD

Note: Alternative selection criteria could include efficiency, effectiveness, cost or innovation.

Step 5: Organize the scoring process

Ensure that every member of your evaluation team understands their role in the scoring process, whether they are part of the core team or a subject matter expert who is helping to score only a section of the incoming proposals. Go over the expectations for each scoring criterion and what kind of responses would warrant awarding each score in a given range to achieve consistency of standards across the evaluators. Finally, decide on a process for distributing proposals, a timeline for turning over evaluations, and a member to collect all the scorecards.

Step 6: Collect and analyze scores

Collection and analysis is the final step to scoring proposals. Review every individual scorecard for arithmetic errors. Aggregate all individual scores to calculate a final score for each candidate firm, either by using an average or a sum. The evaluation committee can then compare the aggregate score of each outside counsel firm against other candidates and select the final candidate.

CHECKLIST:
- ☑ Tailor the complexity of the scoring process to the importance and particular requirements balanced against the availability of time and resources.
- ☑ Consider planning the scoring methodology before sending out the RFP to ensure agreement among stakeholders about relative priority assignment and improve fit between proposal and evaluation.
- ☑ Use each RFP scorecard and scoring process as a learning opportunity to enhance the efficiency of the next iteration.

A STEP-BY-STEP NEGOTIATION PROCESS

In addition to specific pricing questions to be asked in the RFP, the negotiation process will likely need to include other financial and non-financial elements. The answers will assist in qualifying firms and accelerating the negotiation process. Consider the firms' written responses to be the early stage of negotiations.

Some of the non-financial elements to discuss with firms include:

- Commitment to detailed matter planning and budgeting as a way to manage the number and distribution of hours before they are worked by the firm
- Coverage by the firm for each legal specialty, for various levels of partner/associate/paralegal experience, and by jurisdiction
- Expertise and availability of the law firm's team members at all levels of experience
- Service level guarantees with key performance indicators, covering all offices of the firm as well as the allocation of work by primary firms to secondary firms
- A relationship partner accountable for all aspects of the firm's professional and financial performance
- Acceptance of the transfer of administrative and management reporting from the company to primary and coordinating firms as a way to minimize the company's investment in infrastructure.

Some of the financial elements to cover with the RFP and in meetings with firms include:

- The organization's preferred staffing distributions by category of work
- Use of alternative fee arrangements

- Prices and related conditions/discounts for the work proposed by the firm
- Stability of prices over the RFP reference period
- Fees for performance and/or innovation as part of hybrid alternative fee arrangements
- Admissibility of disbursements
- Speed of payment and its relationship to price
- Annual review and adjustment mechanisms based on work type and volumes

(1) FIRST ROUND ELIMINATIONS

The project manager should prepare two reports for the working group. These are useful guides to the other members as you read all the proposals. The reports are a Qualitative Analysis of the Responses to the RFP, including a score for each firm and a Financial Analysis of the Responses to the RFP. Prepare the financial analysis for any discussions with law firms and providers and before any provisional allocations of work to firms or providers.

The working group should be prepared to eliminate proposals that score less than 75 percent on the qualitative (non-financial) analysis.

At this stage, the project manager should urge the working group to reduce the number of proponents without regard to the financial analysis. It makes little sense to engage with law firms or providers for three or more years when their competitors out-score them significantly on multiple fronts. Keep in mind that in-house counsel prefer a gradual approach to eliminating firms for non-financial reasons rather than on price before negotiations commence.

(2) PROVISIONAL ALLOCATIONS

Law firm proposals should indicate the amount and type of available work that they wish to acquire for each jurisdiction. After having read the proposals and the reports prepared by the project manager, the working group should be ready to provide the specifications for a provisional allocation of work before the first round of negotiations with the remaining firms. For example, in the case of the litigation portfolio for a given region you could allocate 60 percent to Firm A and 10 percent to each of four other firms or providers. The project manager then costs the allocation using each firm's initial pricing proposal.

Attention: Do not share this information with the law firms or providers. However, it represents the projected legal spend for each portfolio of work prior to the start of negotiations. It also illustrates any gap with the financial targets set out in the agreed sourcing program.

Some legal departments may be reticent to develop provisional allocations. In such cases, the project manager can prepare an allocation based on historical usage patterns, the proposed pricing of the firms remaining after the first elimination round, and the results of the financial and non-financial analyses. Share this allocation and costing with the members of the working group to serve as a baseline for the first round of negotiations.

Prepare provisional allocations and costing after the first elimination round as well as after each round of negotiations.

PRACTICE TIPS:
The Project Manager should cost at least three provisional allocations of the legal work:
- ☑ One after the first elimination round
- ☑ The second after initial negotiations with law firms and providers
- ☑ The final one after negotiations are completed

(3) IN-PERSON NEGOTIATIONS

Law firms and providers invest considerable resources to prepare comprehensive proposals for legal services, especially for multi-year portfolios of legal work. For your first round of negotiations, face-to-face may be preferable, web-based virtual meetings can be almost as effective (and more perhaps more practical, efficient or sustainable) and during the pandemic they have become the norm. Set aside two hours for each meeting with a firm or provider, especially if you need to cover a list of non-financial items and if you plan to depart from the historical pricing model.

Most legal departments consider their primary law firms to be relationship-based professional business arrangements. An in-person meeting recognizes that relationship, acknowledges the work put into the proposal, and allows the working group to better compare each firm's proposal and responses in a compressed time period.

Invite no more than five participants from each of your law firms and providers. These should include:
- ☑ The relationship partner
- ☑ Two or three other partners responsible for primary categories of work such as litigation, and mergers and acquisitions, etc.
- ☑ The firm's head of pricing

The firm should identify its proposed attendees by name and role in the letter accepting the invitation to meet.

Send an agenda to each law firm or provider three to four weeks prior to the meeting to ensure that each participant is available and make certain that all member of your working group are available. Provided that logistics allow it, meet primary firms and legacy firms early in the sequence. Three meetings per day are sufficient to allow pre-meeting briefings, tardiness by group members, breaks and lunch, and the end-of-day briefing of the group. Schedule a secondary firm if a fourth meeting is necessary on a given day.

The project manager should schedule a half-day preparatory meeting for the working group on the first day of law firm meetings to discuss:

- ☑ The two reports: *The Qualitative Analysis of the Response to the RFP* and *The Financial Analysis of the Responses to the RFP* (see Pricing chapter)
- ☑ Costing of preliminary allocations
- ☑ Roles and responsibilities of each member of the working group, with attention to questions different group members should ask
- ☑ Agenda and issues particular to each firm or provider
- ☑ Timeline for the conduct of each meeting
- ☑ 30-minute end-of-day debriefing session

Send a customized meeting agenda, covering the two-hour meeting to each law firm or provider you invited to a first meeting.

SAMPLE MEETING AGENDA
- Welcome from the project manager
- Self-introduction of each person in attendance
- Introduction and purpose of the RFP by the GC or deputy
- Non-financial questions and answers
- Coverage – expertise, availability of partners, associates, and paralegals
- The law firm's/provider's business model
- Relationship management
- Performance and metrics
- Opportunities for innovation
- Technology and collaboration software
- Management and administration
- Review of the financial proposal
- Practice profiles and staffing distributions
- Preferred pricing model and alternative fee arrangements
- Pricing and conditions, price increases
- Disbursements
- Review and adjustment mechanisms

Only list non-financial questions or items on the agenda that are not satisfactorily addressed in the proposal. In some instances, the project manager may ask the firm or provider to address certain points in writing before the meeting. Ask the firm or provider to submit any items it may wish to discuss should these not be covered in your agenda.

(4) THE FIRST MEETING

Discourage your firms and other service providers from making a general presentation lasting more than 15 minutes. Instead, ask them to customize their presentation to the organization's RFP requirements and to address as many of the agenda items as possible.

For the sake of efficiency and effectiveness, the first four agenda items (Non financial Q&As, Coverage, the firm's business model, relationship management) and the presentation should be completed within the first 60 minutes.

The working group's pricing specialist should lead the financial portion of the meeting. Specific changes to the firm's initial pricing proposal are typically requested, and may include:
- ☑ Coverage by jurisdiction
- ☑ Practice patterns and staffing ratios
- ☑ Configuration of alternative fee arrangements
- ☑ Annual rate and/or price increases
- ☑ Discounts and related conditions

Firms can rely on a mix of variables to offer more favorable prices for the RFP reference period.

At this stage, the organization can suggest a specific target and price together with the relevant conditions, such as volumes and categories of work that would have to be met by your organization to achieve it. Experience suggests that this level of specificity yields a better result than asking for a bigger discount.

Many working groups elect to eliminate some firms after the first round of meetings. There are several reasons for this:

- Some firms were met for legacy business and relationship management purposes but with few chances of work in the future.
- A new firm or provider was invited to propose but did not align well with the legal department members of the working group.

- A firm's or provider's responses to the non-financial and financial discussions offered little chance of significant work allocation in the future.
- The projections for the cost of services will fall outside of the range acceptable to your organization.

The project manager should request a reduced list of eligible firms from the working group to limit the number of participants for the final negotiations. The project manager should also ask the firms or providers for a revised financial proposal within two or three days. This is often done in the form of revised spreadsheets or detailed in a cover letter. The firms or providers should also answer any non-financial questions raised during the meeting. It is not unusual for the firm's or provider's head of pricing to request access to the working group's pricing specialist while preparing revised prices and terms.

PRACTICE TIPS:
☑ The first round of negotiations with firms should be in person. The number of firms invited will likely be reduced from the number submitting proposals. The working group should readily achieve consensus at this stage.
☑ Invite no more than five law firm or provider representatives, including the head of pricing. Ask them to provide names and roles several days before the meeting.
☑ Send a customized agenda to each firm or provider with a selection of items three to four weeks prior to meeting. Ask the firm or provider if they have items to add.
☑ Legal department representatives of the working group should require no more than the first hour of the meeting to lead the non-financial discussions.

- ☑ The working group's pricing specialist leads the financial discussions.
- ☑ The project manager outlines the remainder of the organization's legal sourcing process.
- ☑ Eliminate any firms as a result of this round of meetings.
- ☑ The project manager requests a brief revised proposal from the remaining firms to be submitted within two to three days.

(5) EVALUATING THE REVISED PROPOSALS AND FINAL NEGOTIATIONS

Once the revised proposals or letters have been received, the project manager prepares a brief summary for the working group with a costing of the remaining firms based on the previous allocation or if a new allocation is available, a revised provisional allocation by jurisdiction and category. The summary may include recommendations from the project manager for a different allocation to achieve improved discount thresholds and organization targets.

Alternatively, the project manager and the working group members may decide to initiate a final round of negotiations with one or more of the remaining firms. This round is likely to be primarily financial. In-person discussions are not necessary for this. Instead, one representative of the legal department, the project manager, and the organization's legal pricing specialist can arrange a video call with each firm or provider.

At this point, the organization should be prepared to suggest a provisional allocation of work to each firm or provider in exchange for final and best pricing offers incorporating alternative fee arrangements, fees for performance and innovation, limits to annual increases, as well non-financial arrangements with primary firms. It should be emphasized that provisional allocations can only be revised once the working group considers each of the law firm responses. Allocations will influence each firm's resource allocation, pricing, and workflow management all the while remaining provisional rather than guaranteed.

(6) ALLOCATIONS

Once all the revised proposals and related correspondence are on hand, the working group should meet again to review its planned allocations and costing. Finalize adjustments at this stage. The project manager can then forward Terms of Engagement/Master Service Agreements (MSA) to each firm or provider.

ADMINISTRATIVE ARRANGEMENTS

Accelerated terms of payment in the context of non-hourly fee arrangements typically will leverage a lower overall price. There are examples where anticipated volumes of work are pre-paid and fees reconciled on a quarterly or annual basis.

MSAs and partnering arrangements that cover three to five years cannot accurately anticipate the volume and distribution of work for each year. Variations by complexity and jurisdiction are inevitable. Agreements should include both retrospective and prospective annual review mechanisms. Adjustment to price may be appropriate when work allocation falls outside of an agreed range.

Not all legacy law firms are retained through a sourcing process. It may be necessary to leave certain matters and hours with these firms in the first year while allocating work to successful firms.

PRACTICE TIPS:
- ☑ Prepare a summary of the revised proposals after the first round of meetings with a new costing of the revised work allocation.
- ☑ Conduct a second round of negotiations on select issues with the remaining firms and providers, using video conferencing and a reduced working group for efficiency.
- ☑ Suggest a provisional allocation to certain firms or providers as may be needed to achieve your financial objectives.
- ☑ Prepare another work allocation and costing for the working group once all discussions are completed with firms and providers. The working group should revise/finalize the allocation and pricing at this time.
- ☑ Consider how accelerated payment terms can leverage lower overall prices for legal work.
- ☑ Ensure that the MSAs with law firms and other providers allow for an annual review and adjustment mechanism especially when AFAs are in place.
- ☑ Account for transitional provisions in work allocation.

VALUE TESTS

Several tests can be used to gauge the value your organization can secure from its law firms and providers. The project manager should apply the tests once negotiations with the firms and providers are completed. The results are then shared with other internal stakeholders.

TEST 1: DEMAND FORECASTING

☑ There is a detailed forecast of the demand for internal and external counsel with information other than budget.

☑ The forecast is prepared each year, monitored quarterly and year-to-date.

☑ The forecast is shared with the organization's executive leadership team and with members of the legal department.

TEST 2: LEGAL PROJECT MANAGEMENT

☑ There is a commitment to legal project management (LPM) and budgets for all matters over a certain threshold (e.g. over 50 hours).

☑ LPM should cover phases, tasks, assumptions, probability of success, optimal staffing, hours, schedule, and prices by phase.

☑ Firms/providers and the legal department are both proficient in LPM.

☑ Firms/providers and the legal department each have financial incentives to achieve LPM success.

TEST 3: PREFERRED PRACTICE PATTERNS

☑ Staffing distributions/practice patterns have been agreed with preferred firms for each category of legal work.

TEST 4: PRACTICE PATTERNS AND FEES LINKED

☑ Compliance with profiles is tied to fee arrangements

TEST 5: COMMITMENT TO AFAs

- ☑ The legal department is proficient in AFAs.
- ☑ There is a formal plan to eliminate hourly-based fees within two years.
- ☑ Fee arrangements include a component for performance of regular and exceptional work.
- ☑ There is a financial incentive for firms to embrace alternative fee arrangements.

TEST 6: FINANCIAL AND OTHER PERFORMANCE TARGETS IN PLACE

- ☑ There is a target to reduce external spend by [e.g. 20] percent from projected levels for the RFP reference period.
- ☑ The plan reflects the demand forecast and progressive practices in retaining counsel.
- ☑ The plan does not trade quality for savings.
- ☑ The plan respects at least four key performance indicators: effectiveness, efficiency, innovation, and cost management.
- ☑ Fees are tied to a balanced use of these performance indicators

NEGOTIATE PRICE

A common perception among in-house counsel is that Legal Procurement is entirely focused on costs. In-house lawyers are often concerned that Legal Procurement will always drive them to the lowest cost provider instead of the best provider. In-house counsel are typically more focused on the best services and their established relationships with outside firms, even if they cost more. Getting the right balancing of costs, quality and efficiency is hence necessary.

All aspects of reaching an effective agreement are interrelated. For example, it is critical for Legal Procurement

131

to be aligned with Legal Ops and in-house counsel. Often there are trust gaps, turf issues, or simply unfamiliarity among teams that must be addressed early on in a negotiation. At the same time, in-house counsel have to be willing to try different firms, especially if it means they will drive more work to a smaller number of vendors/partners, which will result in a better partnership, better service, and volume discounts and/or better pricing.

A common rule of thumb states that organizations spend on average 80 percent of their budgets with 20 percent of their providers. Price will certainly be a priority in a negotiation for the top tier of providers. It has become common for law firms and legal services providers to involve pricing and proposal managers familiar with various business and pricing models. It is now best practice for Legal Procurement to negotiate with firm pricing professionals. They speak the same "language" and can educate one another on available options and priorities.

Bargaining power, especially around pricing and payment terms, is still a factor in many negotiations. But there is an increasing realization that power can shift suddenly and dramatically, meaning that power-play strategies exercised by one party are not useful for the long-term and can come back to hurt you.

Before engaging in negotiations, it is crucial to understand the scope of services you request, the firm's or provider's expertise offered, and the timeline for deliverables. A sole focus on short-term or immediate savings can lead to a decrease in the quality of legal services. Over time, low quality services would likely leave your organization vulnerable to even greater expense.

Many organizations explore AFAs, rather than the traditional billable hour to maximize value and reduce the total cost to serve the organization. It is critical that Legal Procurements understand what each model offers when negotiating pricing.

Current best practice in the legal industry favors non-hourly fees for most categories and complexities of work. Generally speaking, alternative fee arrangements stimulate and reward effectiveness, efficiency and innovation in legal services provided there is a measurable contribution for each of these.

In your RFP you should ask questions about both financial and non-financial elements. The answers will assist in qualifying firms and accelerating the negotiation process. Consider the firms' and providers' written responses to be the early stage of negotiations.

Some of the non-financial elements to discuss with firms include:

- A commitment to detailed matter planning and budgeting as a way to manage the number and distribution of hours before they are worked by the firm.
- Coverage by the firm for each legal specialty, for various levels of partner/associate/paralegal experience, and by jurisdiction.
- The expertise and availability of the law firm's team members at all levels of experience.
- Service level guarantees with key performance indicators, covering all offices of the firm as well as the allocation of work by primary firms to secondary firms.
- A relationship partner accountable for all aspects of the firm's professional and financial performance.

- Acceptance of the transfer of administrative and management reporting from the organization to primary and coordinating firms as a way to minimize the organization's investment in infrastructure.

Some of the financial elements to cover with the RFP and in meetings with firms include:

- Preferred staffing distributions by category of work
- Use of alternative fee arrangements
- Prices and related conditions/discounts for the work proposed by the firm
- Stability of prices over the RFP reference period
- Fees for performance and / or innovation as part of hybrid alternative fee arrangements
- Admissibility of disbursements
- Speed of payment and its relationship to price
- Annual review and adjustment mechanisms based on work type and volumes

PRACTICE TIPS:
- ☑ Ensure that the non-financial elements negotiated include matter budgets; coverage and expertise; service level guarantees; relationship management; the targeted use of technology, and the transfer of administrative and management reporting functions to primary firms.
- ☑ Ensure that the financial elements to be negotiated include pricing using AFAs as the predominant fee arrangement; the firm's preferred share of work by category and jurisdiction; the firm's preferred staffing distribution if different from the organization's; fees for performance and/or innovation; the conditions related to more favorable pricing; and the applicable review and adjustment mechanisms.

Pricing negotiations can be highly complex and challenging. They must be based on solid historical data and projections given current and anticipated conditions. Trust, goodwill, and collaboration will make the discussion go smoother.

LEGAL SOFTWARE AND SYSTEMS

Total Cost of Ownership (TCO) needs to be understood when negotiating value and the "right price" for minimum risk, when buying legal technology. A TCO analysis includes determining the direct and indirect costs of an acquisition and operational costs. The purpose of determining the TCO is to help make clear decisions when it comes to pricing. It shifts the focus of the money/value paradigm by prioritizing value and managing cost.

Your TCO calculations can include many factors. They should include both one-time and ongoing costs.

ONE-TIME COSTS
- Hardware
- Accessories
- Installation costs
- Taxes
- Software with a one-time-only license fee

ONGOING COSTS
- Software that requires license renewals
- IT support and maintenance costs
- Hardware upgrades
- Any lost productivity related to unexpected downtime
- User training and education

Break down the costs into as much detail as possible when initially quoting so that you can avoid the potential risk of hidden costs and can effectively benchmark proposals against one another. To do so, ensure that your RFP has detailed pricing information. This will also help alleviate pricing-related disputes later on in the relationship with your providers.

CHECKLIST:
- ☑ It is best practice for Legal Procurement to work directly with the provider's pricing specialist.
- ☑ Procurement should be involved in the development of the legal budget from start to finish. Ideally, all stakeholders, including client and provider teams should collaboratively map current and future pricing plans. Do not forget to include trigger points to reduce or increase pricing as events occur.
- ☑ Have a timeline in place for implementation. If you need work to be done more quickly, factor that into pricing to maintain reasonableness.

PAYMENT TERMS

Negotiation of payment terms up front is important to avoid cash flow problems later. Effectively negotiating payment terms is often a matter of bargaining power: A large client will hold substantial bargaining power and can leverage his/her position to obtain longer windows within which to pay its bills. The same is true for providers with large market share compared to new providers. Clients wanting to negotiate an immediate change in payment terms (e.g. from net 60 days to net 90 days) depend on the provider and his/her market power as well as their desire to continue the partnership.

For some projects, particularly those involving legal software and systems, it may be appropriate to pay a certain percentage upfront as an initial investment. For other projects, such as the provision of legal services, it may be appropriate to pay after the services are rendered.

When negotiating payment terms for legal goods and services, consider:
- How much should be paid to the firm or legal services provider?
- When should those amounts be paid?

INCREMENTAL PAYMENT SCHEMES

Negotiating a split payment system benefits your firms or providers by offering cash up front to begin investment in your requirements. It benefits you by allowing to maintain a higher level of working capital and to manage risk during the life of the project. Discuss the mechanics of a split payment model in conjunction with pricing because an offer of a larger payment upfront can often generate some leverage to reduce the price.

Under incremental payment plans, the options can include 30/70 or 50/50: Legal Procurement can negotiate to pay providers 30 percent up front with 70 percent remaining due upon completion, or it can be half up-front with the remainder upon completion. The percentage splits could vary depending unique circumstance and market conditions.

Another consideration should be when a payment is made, particularly upon completion of a project or the delivery of goods and services. Often, an organization's predefined and optimal payment term is net 90 days from the receipt of an approved invoice. If a provider wants payment under a shorter time frame, customers should consider net 60 or net 45 days, but should also consider incentives for early payments. Early payment discounts (such as "2 percent/10 net 45") can improve a client's profit margins and commercial credit levels. Consistent early payments can also give firms and providers with greater flexibility in negotiating future transactions.

When negotiating payment terms ensure that the mechanics of invoicing approval and early payment discounts (whether offered as an account credit or potentially as a quarterly check), are explicitly outlined and understood between all parties concerned.

It is of crucial importance to correctly collect and analyze historical data on pricing and payment terms as well as other negotiated terms and conditions. A comprehensive approach will help in analyzing risk if all stakeholders are engaged in dealing with and forecasting economic, political and societal conditions.

NEGOTIATE TERMS AND CONDITIONS

When negotiating terms and conditions, be clear about your objectives as well as your least acceptable alternatives for each term and condition. Be aware that your "least acceptable" terms and conditions might be highly acceptable terms and conditions to others. Hence, a degree of flexibility and unbiased thinking is needed to successfully build strategic partnerships for the long-term.

Be sure to understand your organization's preferred terms and conditions as well as the meaning and function of these terms to successfully negotiate and employ them in a commercial context. Understand the precedents: how set terms and conditions impact agreements with other providers or previous/follow-on agreements with the existing provider.

The following terms and conditions are critical to risk management over the life of the relationship between client and provider and need to be addressed:

- Confidentiality
- Indemnification
- Damages
- Arbitration and Dispute Resolution
- Force Majeure

Decide whether a broad or narrow clause will best serve the interests of your organization. This may be beneficial to ensure that all disputes arising out of or relating to the contract are submitted for arbitration. Such a broad clause offers you the opportunity to avoid formal litigation in court, which can be lengthy and expensive for all parties involved. On the other hand, an opposing side may desire to exclude certain disputes, those that are collateral or peripheral to the agreement itself, from arbitration.

Choose the seat (or "situs") of arbitration wisely. Particularly in the international context, this decision is of singular importance. The seat will determine the procedural law for the arbitration and the role of local courts within relation to the proceedings. When negotiating the seat of arbitration, consider the ease of access for both parties, the availability of arbitrators, and judicial experience levels. Also be aware of the various arbitration bodies available, their rules, and how arbitral proceedings occur.

MASTER SERVICES AGREEMENTS

Client organizations increasingly use Master Services Agreements (MSAs) (also often called Master Retention Agreements, MRAs) when they contract with a large number of (preferred) providers. MSAs comprise the common or basic Terms and Conditions for all providers, thus avoiding the need to negotiate each and every term for each contract. Individual contracts can then be crafted with the unique terms needed for each provider.

It is considered best practice for legal departments to have an MSA in place with their firms and providers as part of the overall outside counsel management program. Having all firms operate under the same agreement simplifies administration for the in-house legal team. MSAs typically outline:

- Confidentiality
- Conflicts of Interest
- Media/PR Rights (such as logo usage)
- Governing Law/Dispute Resolution
- Discount arrangements

MSAs highlight important department initiatives, such as diversity and inclusion, and how the client expects firms to participate. They also feature "Billing Guidelines" that detail what the organization will and will not pay for.

It is critical that all providers operate on the same Billing Guidelines for audit, tracking and reporting purposes. For example, if the firms use different guidelines for different practice areas, it is difficult for lawyers to remember the various nuances and therefore cannot markdown the invoice accordingly. It is also difficult for firms that handle matters in multiple practice areas to manage to different sets of billing guidelines.

In addition, most electronic billing (eBilling) systems cannot accommodate multiple sets of guidelines and therefore cannot properly flag billing violations. It is essential to lay out how you want your firms to submit invoices. Your eBilling system can be set up to track all the savings achieved using your Billing Guidelines, an important metric to capture.

Depending on the jurisdiction you work on, reference Uniform Task Based Management System (UTBMS) task codes. UTBMS is a series of codes used to classify legal services performed by a legal provider in an electronic invoice submission. UTBMS codes are widely used in the United States. (Go to www.utbms.com for further information.)

Also learn more about the newer Legal Matter Specification Standard (LMSS) (www.sali.org). LMSS comprises standardized code sets that define the "common language" for describing different aspects of legal matters as well as a structure or database format that defines how the codes, descriptions and values relate to each other. In other jurisdictions, including many EMEA countries, you might need to use descriptive invoices for the time being.

When setting up an MSA for the first time, understand what is industry best practice. Work with one or two of your top firms to understand what is reasonable with them, and then use that as a template for other firms. This can make the process easier by identifying and fixing, possible controversial or contentious parts of the contract early on. Keep the MSA form simple and as short as possible, no more than two to three pages (without the addendums) and make sure your internal stakeholders are aligned: Legal, Procurement, Finance, and Accounting.

While having an MSA set up is current industry best practice, it is also a heavy lift to get all of your firms onto one agreement, especially if there is not strong support and project management from Legal Procurement. Again, remember that all stakeholders involved should help during this process.

If you do not have the support or bandwidth to implement an organization-wide MSA process, focus on your top ten or 20 providers and set up the MSA with them. At a minimum, ensure that your Billing Guidelines are sent to all of your providers and make sure they understand these as non-negotiable. Make it very clear that invoicing you means they have accepted your Billing Guidelines. You could also set up a Matter Specific Engagement Letter for each matter opened with a provider. This could be a very short form describing:

- The name/description of the matter
- A conflict of interest clause
- Obligations the provider is agreeing to by managing this matter
- Your Billing Guidelines if you have not sent them to the provider

Once you have taken these steps, put protocols into place for measuring success. This includes regular reporting:

- ☑ **Internal reporting** will show cost savings generated by the program in terms of overall hourly rate discounts, volume discounts, proper billing practices (For example, the eBilling system shows billing violations that should be reported).
- ☑ **External reporting** on the percentage of firms on the "preferred provider list" versus firms used that are not on that list. The usage of "non-preferred providers" should diminish over time as they may continue to finish current cases, but non-preferred providers should not get new work.

Conduct law firm scorecard reporting on the quality of the firms you are using. Your scorecard should measure accessibility, ease of doing business, substantive experience, results, and budget performance. Share your scorecards with your internal stakeholders as well as with your respective providers. It is best practice to meet at least annually with each firm to discuss how to improve the partnership. Use this time to provide them with feedback and ask for feedback in return. The firms should be coming to you with data and ideas on how to improve the relationship and the work being done.

MANAGE FIRMS AND PROVIDERS

SUPPLIER RELATIONSHIP MANAGEMENT

Supplier Relationship Management (SRM) in the context of legal services is strategically planning for and managing all interactions with your firms and other legal services providers to maximize the value of those interactions for both parties involved. SRM is particularly important in times of intensified competition in the legal services sector on the one hand and increased cost pressure on legal departments on the other.

Supplier development is based on the idea of developing strategic, long-term relationships with select firms and providers. To be able to strategically develop a provider, you need to define and agree on specific development goals. Developing providers is a tool to close gaps in a provider's performance but also to challenge existing and new providers to be innovative and come up with improvements.

Establish supplier development goals in areas you conduct performance evaluations. Here are some examples:

- **Qualitative development goal** - Developing competency in a particular area of expertise: If you have two firms matching your requirements where one is more cost efficient but missing a certain area of expertise, you could consider developing a provider towards that competency to benefit from their efficiency gain in the long run.
  Another example could be substituting a certain percentage of the provider's services with technology in order to raise efficiencies.

- **Financial development goal** - Developing a provider towards more pro-active and efficient pricing models. This could be fixed fee models or developing an efficient budget monitoring process.

NOTE: From your provider's point of view, there also might be areas that you as a client could improve upon, such as being more transparent in decision making, communicating changes early on or being more transparent on financial goals. When developing strategic long-term partnerships with select firms and providers, you may want to develop performance plans together that you both agree on. Make them an integral part of your annual review meetings.

BENEFITS OF SUPPLIER RELATIONSHIP MANAGEMENT

- ☑ **Increased efficiency**: Intensive cooperation between client and firm or provider will lead to open communication about mutual expectations and ideas for joint cooperation. Analysis of existing processes is understood on both sides as optimization of the same and investment in the relationship. The longer and more intensive the cooperation, the greater the trust and efficiencies that will benefit every matter.
- ☑ **Reduced external cost for legal services**: A long-term strategic partnership has significant impact on the price the client pays, as firms and providers are potentially more willing to deviate from their standard rates, agree to AFAs, and provide additional free value-added services (such as pre-matter planning sessions). Clients who perceive to receive value, are also more likely to establish a trusting and long-term relationship.

☑ **Reduced internal costs and effort:** If the client has already invested in a strategic relationship and it has proven to be successful, it is highly recommended that the considerable effort involved in an RFP for a new selection of external providers should not be carried out at extremely short intervals, unless market developments and new services and products make this necessary. Even if a new provider promises lower costs, the long-term relationships established with strategic partners generate more value than possible short-term gains from lower rates.

☑ **Performance improvement:** The ability to monitor the performance of strategic providers and to have a positive impact on their performance also contributes to efficiency gains such continuous improvement in cooperation and an increase in the quality of the services provided.

☑ **Risk and Compliance:** Effective supplier relationship management also offers protection in terms of risk and compliance. Failure to comply with laws and regulations can, at best, result in heavy fines, but at worst have an impact on your organization's reputation, damage to your brand and lead to lost sales.

A number of factors can influence the quality of Supplier Relationship Management, including:

Establishing formal agreements: Having formal agreements in place influences the development and quality of the relationship between your organization and your firms and providers.

Create a common understanding about:
- Conditions (e.g. Billing Guidelines)
- Mutual expectations (framework agreement without acceptance obligations or panel agreement with a clear focus on one legal area). Keep in mind that too high or wrong expectations can lead to demotivation and have an impact on mutual trust, commitment and the relationship between the client and their supplier.

Selecting the right suppliers: An important success factor for your SRM is selecting the right suppliers for strategic relationships as your supplier relationship program will tie up resources. The more supplier partners you utilize, the more difficult it will be to maintain the level of communication and collaboration and to build the trust required for successful Supplier Relationship Management.

Identify the selection criteria: Consider how value is created for your organization as well as performance, service portfolio and innovation potential.

Splitting roles and responsibilities: Make sure that all parties involved have a clear understanding of their respective roles and responsibilities. For example:
- Who hosts a strategic event?
- Who is responsible and the sole contact person in tendering processes?
- Who participates in the decisions making process and who is the final decision maker?
- Who is responsible for and conducts annual review meetings?

Also address the handling of critical issues that could have a negative influence on the working relationship between outside counsel and in-house counsel.

If roles and responsibilities are not defined in advance, it can become a challenge for cooperation between the legal department and supporting functions as well as in the external image towards suppliers.

Communicating based on mutual trust: Trust and communication are essential in a strategic partnership and key to the success of any relationship management. A certain degree of transparency in mutual processes also creates trust and understanding. Trust is also built through open communication and regular two-way feedback helps to create this transparency.

IMPLEMENT A SUPPLIER RELATIONSHIP MANAGEMENT PROGRAM

To establish an effective SRM program, take the following steps:

- ☑ **Segment suppliers**: Identify the level of importance of each firm and legal service provider.
- ☑ **Develop a value map**: Invite key stakeholders and find answers to the following questions: What are your goals? What do you want to achieve with the selected legal service providers? How can they contribute the desired value? Do not lose sight of the win-win approach.
- ☑ **Define individual measures**: What measures do you want to take to create further development, process improvements, and innovation? Determine how you want to deal with providers who no longer meet the criteria in the future.
- ☑ **Set up the operational foundation**: What tools and processes should be used to ensure a successful relationship management program?

149

☑ **Stakeholder engagement**: Present the drafted concept to your stakeholders. Define roles and responsibilities, and share feedback. You need to have a final mutually agreed-upon concept for your relationship management program.

☑ **Approach select suppliers**: Decide with your providers how the previously defined values can be developed. Define clear individual goals.

SUPPLIER RELATIONSHIP MANAGEMENT STRATEGY – MEASURES OVERVIEW

Operational SRM focuses on all data that forms the basis for tactical relationship management with your key firms and providers. Aim to get real-time information. This is particularly relevant with regard to spend data and invoice data to avoid a distorted view in reporting. During regular project review meetings, discuss major service and quality improvements as well as any potential amendments and changes to the service scope.

Tactical SRM supports achieving your strategic goals in specific legal projects. An example would be if your organization communicates its goal of improving legal budget management with a technical solution at the external Council Day. Within the scope of a specific legal project, one of the preferred suppliers offers legal project management supported by such a technical solution. This solution is then tested as a pilot within the specific project and later purchased as a legal tech solution.

Strategic SRM measures help define what you want to achieve in the long term when cooperating with your suppliers. It focuses on enabling supplier development, improving established processes, and the joint development of innovations.

Start with an Annual Review Meeting with each law firm or provider. Potential topics you should discuss include spend development, recent project quality issues and how these could be solved. You could also give feedback why the provider was not awarded some projects and what the decisive points were for awarding others. Give each other feedback and share your expectations. This will have significant impact on your relationship.

PRACTICE TIPS:

☑ Organize WORKSHOPS on specific topics, such as pricing, digitalization, and legal technology developments. These also enable the exchange among providers. Use the opportunity to get to learn about new products and services and identify opportunities to work together. This is also an opportunity to recruit participants for project groups to drive forward organization-specific topics. Providers will be most willing to participate and invest their time if a close relationship already exists or if the organization has just been acquired as a new client for a comparatively large project and providers can hope to intensify the new client relationship.

☑ Organize an EXTERNAL COUNSEL DAY for legal services. To send the right message and be successful both internally and externally, your GC should host the event. Welcome your providers (current and potential) and introduce your organization. Increase the value of your relationship with your providers by being transparent about your goals and expectations.

151

☑ Share with them information such as:
- What are the short-term and long-term goals of the organization and the legal department?
- What do you expect from your legal service providers?
- What solutions do you need?
- What challenges do you foresee in the future?

Create space for networking between in-house counsel (and other decision makers) and outside counsel. Use the time for brief workshops (e.g. engagement processes, legal questions etc.) and end the day with the good feeling of having created added value for the organization by investing in the relationship with your key suppliers.

To establish a successful supplier relationship management program work with your firms and suppliers, exchange information and discuss new ideas. Focus on how you can create long-term value for each other and identify opportunities to achieve this goal. Use new developments of your legal service providers to pay into the "efficiency account" and support them to establish these developments in the market. Invest in networks to generate mutual benefits.

PERFORMANCE MANAGEMENT

The services of law firms and legal services providers are essential to the health and wellbeing of an organization and how these firms perform impact how your organization performs itself. Clients cannot leave performance to trust, it needs to be measured and developed.

Supplier Performance Management is a two-layered, structured approach to managing and developing providers towards certain goals while also improving your own performance. The layers consist of measuring:

- Overall provider performance
- Project/Matter performance

The two layers create a holistic approach to supplier performance management. In combination with relationship management they should be part of any strategic supplier management program.

TWO-LAYERED SUPPLIER PERFORMANCE MANAGEMENT APPROACH

Overall provider performance management: For a long-term relationship to grow the value for both, client and legal supplier, it is essential to measure the provider's overall performance. Conduct it annually. Overall provider performance management typically includes:

- ☑ The sum of the provider's project performances
- ☑ Development of provider performance over the course of several projects and the relationship
- ☑ The provider's risk management
- ☑ The provider's reputation

153

- ☑ The provider's fit for your organization's strategy and reputation
- ☑ The provider's management of performance issues
- ☑ The provider's development and innovation of its services

Some providers handle all of their projects and resources well while others rely on great individuals, but overall do not sustain constant quality across all mandates.

Use your providers' project performances to calculate their performance based on the ratings of their performances during the previous year. To get a more complete picture of your provider's performance, also consider their performance over a specific time, especially if you look for long-term strategic partnership with select firms.

Another dimension you want to assess is a provider's risk management. This includes the provider's financial stability, talent pipeline, flexibility and adaptability as well as innovation potential.

Finally, consider the provider's reputation or market behavior. This is particularly important in the legal space when handling sensitive cases with public impact. A firm can be perfect for you on a working basis but does not strategically fit to your organization. Looking beyond project performance shifts the perspective from a project-oriented steering to a long-term partnership approach with key firms and providers.

Project/Matter performance management is key to operational excellence and successful handling of matters. You should assess project/matter performance on an on-going basis.

Project performance is key in the short-term perspective and focused on your satisfaction with your provider's services during a project. It is best practice to measure pre-defined KPIs such as staying in budget, reaction times, lead times, iteration rounds etc.

Project/Matter performance management typically includes:

- ☑ Quality of services
- ☑ Integrity/Reliability of team during the project
- ☑ Financial efficiency during the project

To evaluate project/matter performance, you want to collect both quantitative data as well as qualitative data. Qualitative data collection (e.g. interviewing in-house counsel or the law firm and collecting comments and feedback) typically takes more time or effort than the quantitative data collection. As time constrains and heavy workloads are often a challenge, you may opt to focus on collecting quantitative data to get a quick insights into whether the project is coming along smoothly or whether it has hit any roadblocks. To get quick insight but keep the effort at a minimum and still allow for regular evaluations of performance ask in-house counsel the following three questions, using a four-star scale.

1. Evaluate the quality of services delivered (successful closing of matter/project, competence of available staff, constructive work attitude/proactive behavior, out of the box/innovative ideas)

2. Evaluate the legal supplier's reliability & willigness to collaborate (e.g. flexibility in changing environments, crisis management, collaboration with inhouse teams, sub-contractors and other suppliers, adherence to the contractual agreements, follows agreed processes (e.g. agreed ways of communication, reporting mechanisms, budget & scope change management)

3. Evaluate the financial performance of the legal supplier (adherence to agreed budgets, general pricing, intelligent fee structures, efficient staffing & use of technology)

4. Would you like to add any comments to your evaluation?

Type your answer..

SAMPLE PROJECT PERFORMANCE EVALUATION

Note: Using an even number on the rating scale ensures that the evaluating person has to select a negative or positive tendency. However, you can select your scale but make sure that you define the different rating options so they lead to meaningful feedback.

156

Conduct project evaluations right after closing a matter/project or during the closing phase. For a robust performance management process, make performance evaluation an integral part of the project cycle and project management. Such assessment or debriefing at the end of each matter/project ensures that your organization can learn from the experience.

For longer projects (often defined as longer than six months) you may want to evaluate the performance also during the project, at certain milestones. This ensures that issues and poor performance are spotted early on when there is still time to mitigate and influence the outcome of the matter. For such longer projects, consider the following standard evaluation cycles:

- ☑ **First-Assessment**: Start with a first evaluation at the beginning of the project right after a sufficient orientation phase to set the team and project on the right track, exchanging expectations and setting the guardrails.
- ☑ **Mid-Project**: To check on the project halfway and to see if everything is running smoothly, conduct a mid-project evaluation. For shorter projects, the first-evaluation and the mid-project evaluation could be combined.
- ☑ **Final Review**: The final evaluation should be mandatory, independent of the length of your project assessing how the project went overall.

You may want to collect feedback from your providers on your performance, making it a two-way street or 360-degree performance review. Beware that legal service providers still do not regularly ask for feedback. However, for both sides evaluating areas of strengths and weaknesses can help detect areas for improvement and initiate corresponding improvement processes. For example, give each other feedback on questions such as:

- ☑ Was the scope of the mandate sufficiently described?
- ☑ Was a pricing proposal based on this description possible?
- ☑ Was the deadline for submitting the proposal reasonable?
- ☑ How were the designated contact persons reachable for questions?

You can also use annual review meetings to discuss results and evaluations with your firms and providers in more depth and collect feedback or have project reviews to ensure smooth running. Annual reviews are part of an overall provider evaluation and go deeper than a single project review.

Reviewing overall supplier performance is a much more time intensive approach than the ongoing project evaluations. It is a deep dive into your firms' or providers' general set up, strategic direction, and performance. Such deep dives make sense with firms and providers you identified as strategic partners, with whom you want to continue to work with and grow your business.

You may want to evaluate your providers on a yearly cycle or depending on your number of suppliers, every two to three years. Consider linking a provider's overall performance review to your contract renewal or firm selection process.

Start your evaluation with collecting data in your organization as well as from the firm or provider. The process should include a meeting between you and your provider reviewing your findings. An open dialog is the basis for a healthy relationship with your providers.

PROCESS TEMPLATE

DATA COLLECTION

- ☑ Project performance: Project evaluations; development over several years
- ☑ Risk management: Financial data; strategic development; talent pipeline; provider portfolio development
- ☑ Market reputation: Law firm rankings or other benchmarks; press releases

INTERNAL EVALUATION

- ☑ Strategic Fit: Does the portfolio/services of the firm/provider fit your needs? Does the strategic direction of the firm/provider fit your organization's strategy and future needs?
- ☑ Performance: Is the firm's/provider's performance meeting your requirements and expectations?

REVIEW MEETING WITH THE PROVIDER

- ☑ Exchange expectations
- ☑ Openly discuss findings and feedback
- ☑ Define mutual goals and measures for development
- ☑ Agree on follow up reviews and next steps

Performance management is an organizational group effort and part of a complete supplier management approach. In-house counsel holds most of the valuable performance information, in particular how the firms/providers performed on individual matters. However, their view is likely limited to the matters they were responsible for. They may not be aware of the firm's or provider's performance in other matters. That is why it is best practice for Legal Procurement to collect performance data across matters and manage general supplier performance. You can also provide additional data on overall performance, foster the evaluation process and build strategic relationships with providers.

The key to supplier performance management is transparency across the organization on the provider's performance. Only then you will be able to streamline selection and engagement of providers, speak with one voice to a provider and create value through the relationship.

You support in-house counsel by supplying a provider's overall evaluation score, highlighting their areas of expertise, price range etc. It is vital that in-house counsel has access to this information at any time when considering to engage external counsel. Work with your colleagues in the legal department to ensure that you collect provider data they deem important. The more helpful the data is for in-house counsel, the more willing they will be to provide evaluations and participate in review meetings.

Law Firm XYZ	# running projects	$XX spend over the last Year
Cost	Should be used for	Supplier Score
$ - $$$	e. g. standard / highly critical (projects)	★★★✦
Sustainability Score	Preferred for practice area:	Global or Regional?
● ● ●	e. g. M&A, Litigation, Regulatory [...]	e.g. EMEA and US

SAMPLE SUPPLIER PROFILE

Introducing a robust performance management system with your firms and providers will have a positive impact on their performance. Collaboration with your firms and providers requires defining and collecting relevant information in a way that is identical for all your firms or providers of the same type. Your baseline must be uniform to rank your firms and providers. You also need to have a clear approach to promoting or demoting your firms and providers on the basis of results. The results of the regular performance review could be shared amongst your preferred firms and providers and the majority of your work should be given to those who perform best.

Value can be different things to different buyers under different circumstances but is typically defined as a combination of quality and price. And quality is a combination of service and results.

MEASURING VALUE

To assess value, organizations often look at whether their providers hit price requirements that were set out in rates table, RFP responses, quotes or panel charges negotiated. Using this approach to measure performance is a challenge in itself. Does it mean that if a supplier agrees the price you want, that they should score highly for performance for being flexible? What if they delivered in half the time, but were 20 percent more expensive? This metric is only applicable to performance over a long period of time, when you look at inter-period changes and might be measured as a 'percentage price change year-on-year.'

A somewhat more sophisticated approach would be to use price avoidance metrics, e.g. if the first quoted price is $100 and the buyer negotiates it down to $95. That is $5 saving per hour. This price drop potentially results into a large sum when scaled to industrial volumes in a high-spend client. A word of caution: Treat percentage-based metric carefully, as figures are difficult to aggregate when you deal with varying volumes and service values. An absolute number (rather than a percentage) allows for easy accumulation of the final amount. However, Procurement must defend this figure and the $5 saved in the example is not real money that can be used elsewhere as it is "just" cost avoidance.

Instead, consider using total cost of ownership (TCO) models as they attempt to bring more relevance to the costs of operating with a particular firm or provider and as a result are expanded to look at the cost sustained for the entire time period.

MEASURING QUALITY

Measuring quality can also be challenging. At the simplest level, quality relates to "performance to contract." Has the firm or provider delivered the service to the specified level? While in manufacturing you would measure the defects per part or rejected parts per order, in legal services you could measure the service your firms and providers provide to internal clients, and you could build that into your contracts and make payment to your firms and providers partly based upon review. A certain contract percentage could be paid, if the supplier hits a 90 percent approval rating within stakeholder reviews. This is a means to ensure that the firm or provider activities are strictly in line with the requirements of the business.

You can assess your law firms and providers through a range of different measurement tools. The important aspect is to ensure that in whatever metric you select, it needs to reflect the requirements of your organization and incentivize your firms and providers.

QUALITY MANAGEMENT

Quality needs to be addressed in multiple phases of an engagement – from the choice of the right provider to the final evaluation. The challenge you may face is that when Legal Procurement and in-house lawyers discuss quality, they often focus on different aspects. Procurement typically sees quality in the context of "fair value," while in-house counsel tends to focus mostly on legal outcomes. This can lead to conflicting interpretations of the same set of facts. Therefore, different types of quality need to be considered and managed effectively.

ASSESS QUALITY OF WORK

Quality of work can be different things depending on the situation, entailing different consequences for both clients and providers of the service. The quality of work should relate to the proficiency of the service provided.

Clients typically have the quality of the work product in mind when talking about "quality" in legal services. It concerns the output side of the service delivery and disregards both the legal services provider and its resources spent (i.e. staffing, outsourcing, near shoring, etc.). In the absence of conflicting information this should be your default choice when unsure as to which type of quality is concerned. The main concern is whether the work performed corresponds to the expectations you clearly communicated to your provider and whether your provider was responsive to your demands.

Be aware that in legal services, even a good work product that meets the expectations and was executed diligently, may result in a non-desired outcome (i.e. losing a case).

There are numerous factors that may jeopardize a matter and despite good quality of work and work products, things can go wrong. The reasons are often outside their influence on the matter and can stem from a variety of factors that are in all likeliness unknown at the outset of a matter (such as natural disasters, change of public opinion, legislative changes, "force majeure" events etc.). Sometimes such random events cannot be avoided, you therefore have to manage your expectations with regards to the services provided.

Set up a list of both soft (more subjective) and hard (more objective) KPIs. For example, a KPI based on the outcome of a case is purely objective: The case either progresses as expected or it does not. The assessment of the work supplied is mostly objective, as (assuming that expectations were properly communicated at the outset) those can be measured against those expectations. Cooperation between the firm or provider and your organization is fundamentally more difficult to measure, as the quality of that relationship is largely determined on the people involved on both sides. Focus on KPI such as responsiveness, timeliness and politeness (on both sides) to determine whether the cooperation was successful and whether, thereby, the desired quality of service was achieved.

CHECKLIST: Determine which criteria you want to use when evaluating service quality.

- ☑ If you have few objective criteria, give more weight to these objective criteria in the overall evaluation. Subjective criteria tend to skew the evaluation too much based on relationships, and less on criteria such as price or work products.
- ☑ If you use many KPIs, give individual data points lower overall weight, especially if a lot of objective criteria are available. Otherwise the topic becomes a cherry-picking exercise without impact.

Give the gap between "expected result" and "realized result" significant weight. As long as it is communicated clearly at the outset, it takes into account both subjective and objective criteria in a balanced way (no internal counsel would want external counsel to fail, as they are - at least partially - responsible for the matter).

Tie your evaluations to the pricing performance of your providers through a "bonus/malus" system, in the form of contingent fees, or fee models dependent on the achievement of certain (pre-defined) milestones tied to performance (i.e. "reactiveness of 24 hours or less"). Communicate clearly which criteria you take into account when you evaluate quality, as this allows both Legal and Procurement to properly weigh the evaluation.

NOTE: It is practically impossible to remove subjectivity: e.g. if the people involved do not like each other, cooperation will be difficult to master, information flows will be problematic, and thereby, affect the outcome negatively.

When assessing risk, different departments focus on different aspects: Procurement is typically focused on financial and supply risks and Legal focuses on legal risk. For legal services, always take into account all three: financial, supply, and legal risk.

Legal Risk: Different jurisdictions require different "levels of care." This can have a direct impact on your selection of firms and providers. Public enforcement bodies or courts may regard firms and providers differently depending on their reputation, perceived quality of work, etc. For example, selecting a lower-cost provider could be regarded as negligent on the part of your organization, thereby opening up possibilities for litigation and damage claims, even if the outcome compared to the higher cost provider might be the same.

It may be difficult to assess legal risks of an engagement from a purely financial perspective. Nonetheless, a helpful first estimate of the financial value of the legal risk is the difference in price for two firms whose quality of work is equal, but their reputational component is not. The delta between the two corresponds to the risk premium. Discuss this risk premium with your colleagues in the legal department to ensure that the risk premium does not outweigh the legal risks based on the engagement of less pertinent counsel (for example, the litigation risk and an award/fine based on the counsel selection is not smaller than the risk premium, etc.).

Law firms are aware of their reputation and perceived value in such risk-mitigation situations and thereby have bargaining power in the context of these types of engagements. Be aware of these situations but ensure that your organization only pays fair value for these services and avoids undeserved premium prices.

Financial Risk: The insurance industry translates risk into a financial number. Similar to insurance premiums, a risk premium could be seen as a translation of the legal risk the organization is incurring with a given engagement of a law firm. This implies that the fees paid to a firm correspond to the true value the organization measures the services with. However, in practice, this conciliation between the service offered and its financial value to the organization is often difficult, if not impossible. Indeed, the financial risks are often one-sided: The law firm will get paid regardless of the outcome, and mostly regardless of the quality of service delivered. To avoid this, you should balance the incurred financial risk with your providers through appropriate fee arrangements.

Clients often opt for success fees in unknown environments to ensure that the provider they hire remain committed to a given case. However, this only leaves two options: Either the organization has no clear understanding of the case, but the law firm does, thereby having an upside of potentially supra-competitive profits. Or both partners are looking at a black box and have no understanding of the work to be carried out. In the first case, the scoping elaborated by the organization is exceptionally bad, as the law firm has a better understanding of the cases than its client has, in the latter, both will likely be displeased with the outcome, as the firm might have assumed less work, and the client was hoping for a better outcome.

Generally speaking, success fees are obsolete in situations where the firm is expected to deliver a certain outcome (i.e. win a case) and where there is no direct relation between the amount of work the firm puts into the case (e.g. in terms of expertise, work hours, innovation, etc.) needed to deliver that outcome. If a firm accepts success fees as payment for such services, you can assume that the firm possesses historical information that allows it to estimate the amount of work required. This information asymmetry rarely works for the client who ends up overpaying. Instead, you should put more effort into accurately scoping the engagements before discussing fees with firms and then price them jointly with their firms.

Through a comparison of historical data on pricing for certain services, industry overviews, RFP procedures, legal knowledge, and transferability of pricings across matters, Procurement can more accurately predict what the price point for a given service should be.

Take into account both the quality and quantity requirements for the specific engagement. Your pricing arrangement has to make allowances for the possibility of the engagement being more or less complex than assumed. Pricing should account for these issues and standard Procurement tools such as itemized pricing, segmentation and proper comparison can yield significant successes.

The same is true for bespoke agreements reflecting the developments of a specific case (such as time-based payments, installments based on milestones, etc.). In addition, legal risk can and should play a role in the determination of the correct price point as outlined above. Similarly, Procurement needs to ensure that an adjustment mechanism is incorporated in the pricing arrangement to ensure that financial risks are evenly balanced between legal service providers and companies.

Please note that risk management is often used to pretend that most risks can be prevented from happening and that a zero-risk approach is feasible. This is not the case and you should distrust service providers and internal departments claiming to be able to deliver this. Risk management is about establishing guardrails that can be used in case of adverse events (or adverse legal outcomes). The risk is then managed in a way that it is mitigated or contained.

While there are different types of risks, one fundamental difference must be made: Risks that can be reasonably foreseen and those that cannot.

- **Risks that can be reasonably foreseen**: This is an accepted and accounted-for deviation of the overall strategy of procuring and delivering legal services and should not lead to serious issues with regards to pricing and delivery of services. A prime example of such accommodation is fee arrangements that adjust over time based on external factors.

- **Risks that cannot be reasonably foreseen**: You cannot account for events for which you neither know their timely realization nor their impact (both financial and legal) as well as their (possible) ripple effects throughout other areas of activity for your organization. It is therefore even less possible to engage in active risk-management for these types of events, as this would require you to obtain information on the state of the market, the legal environment and the players in each of those that goes beyond what is available. For this reason, such risks can only be mitigated, contained, or provisioned for (to a very limited extent). If adverse events happen, the arrangements made with your provider need to be sufficiently robust to allow both parties to continue working together satisfactorily. Since it is difficult to account for unforeseeable risk, impose guardrails that should be flexible enough to accommodate these situations (for example through pre-agreed methods, pre-agreed billing modalities etc.).

It is crucial to understand guardrails not only from your perspective, but also from your providers' perspective. Either you end up overpaying or your provider ends up losing profitability. The establishment of appropriate guardrails is crucial when deciding on a pricing regime for a given matter. For example, cushion arrangements (i.e. +/- a certain percentage) for fixed fees can balance some risk with regards to monetary adjustments to fees. In the same vein, the introduction of review cycles, coupled with a good faith obligation to negotiations can provide opportunities for fair price finding in situations of limited visibility (such as litigation).

Similarly, negotiating a price menu beforehand enables clients and providers alike to add predictability to their fees/revenues. It permits assessing the fees payable for certain activities in advance, thereby obviating the need to renegotiate fees in case of overruns on one item or under runs on others. This kind of partnering entails detailed negotiations upfront and a candid conversation on expectations in terms of quality and services provided.

As a fallback option, you can agree to use shadow-billing for a certain period of time during the introduction of new fee arrangements, as this allows both you and your providers to verify the actual outcome of their fee arrangement (many firms will shadow-bill anyways for their internal revenue calculations, therefore this is not an unreasonable request).

In addition, the introduction of service level agreements (SLA) for certain types of work ensures that expectations are made explicit and that your provider is required to adhere to them. You can emphasize this through penalties for not adhering. While they are a standard Procurement approach, SLAs have only recently been introduced for legal services. Nonetheless, SLAs are a helpful tool to ensure that the expected quality-of-service is reached or maintained. The guardrails thus established reassure both partners that, depending on engagement development, the compensation is fair and appropriate.

NOTE: In the context of legal services, there is no clear distinction between legal and financial risks. Legal risks may translate into financial risks and financial risks may translate into legal risks if the risk rests on the firm or provider performing the service.

The question you must ask is what the right balance between legal and financial risk should be. There is no easy answer, but Procurement should be aware that lawyers in general tend to be very risk-averse and will likely value legal risks greater than direct financial risks from a law firm engagement. Even on routine engagements they might prefer a firm that can be engaged on bet-the-organization/high-risk work. By contrast, a risk-conscious legal department would also approve newer providers (or even legal tech solutions) for low to mid-level legal risk areas, likely resulting in a more cost conscious solution for the organization.

Be aware of the true financial risk of legal risk (e.g. a lost bellwether trial, which is a test case intended to try a widely contested issue) and take this into account when negotiating appropriate fee arrangements with providers (you may want to pay more for a bellwether trial compared to the similarly intense work following it). This is particularly problematic for Procurement not concerned with quality and value, but only pricing. Hence, take a more holistic view of legal services and verify that the right service is acquired at the right cost, at the right time. This framework is sufficiently robust to ensure that the prices paid correspond to both, fair market value and risk-conscious-behavior.

LEGAL PROJECT MANAGEMENT AND BUDGET MANAGEMENT

Providing legal services based on hourly rates has been associated with a lack of transparency and predictability in terms of cost, time, and quality of a mandate. In the legal services market, pricing used to be mainly determined by the provider of the service. Today, mandates are managed far more efficiently because both clients and their law firms and providers have made legal project management and the associated efficiency and transparency their top priority.

Legal departments are redesigning both processes and pricing models for external legal advice to develop a better understanding of their external legal spend and better control their budgets. Clients invest heavily into a collaborative relationship with their preferred firms and providers to promote innovation and jointly develop technologies that support innovation. Enhanced communication and mutual feedback help to achieve the goals set and are key to success.

Most clients want the pricing estimates to be as accurate as possible and a certain degree of predictability of the costs they will incur for external legal advice. They appreciate the opportunity to retain control over the costs, once work has begun and they value the close cooperation with their selected law firms and the opportunity to invest in existing relationships, drive innovation and mitigate risk through a structured matter management.

It is essential for legal service providers to have a clear understanding of what you need, your objectives and preferences. Optimal planning of matters before starting the actual work on a mandate is crucial. An efficient procedure with regular updates on the status of the proceedings increases the value of the services provided for you. Applying project management to legal matters supports the kind of legal advice that is both client-focused and cost-effective.

Budget management includes both planning at the beginning of a matter and ongoing control. Precise planning at the beginning of a matter enables firms to better manage client expectations, especially with regards to costs and budget. This is also important in light of increasing your ability to manage and respond quickly to changes in the project that may affect scope, deliverables, timeframe or resources. You can minimize risks and mistakes through the precise planning of tasks and resources and efficient working methods.

Legal departments benefit from budget management in a number of ways:

- ☑ Effective internal cost management
- ☑ Increased cost transparency
- ☑ Budget predictability
- ☑ Reduced costs
- ☑ Reduced risks
- ☑ Improved quality management

Budget management also leads to improved efficiency and profitability for your firms and providers. Higher efficiency also increases the processing speed and with it, the profitability of the matter.

This should allow your law firms and providers to offer you (more) attractive pricing, which in turn, should result in an improved possibility of legal spend planning (long-term budget planning), and better financial predictability (which costs will be incurred when). More value leads to more trust and thus to greater client satisfaction - the best foundation for a long-term partnership with benefits for both sides.

Proper budget management also increases your legal department's credibility with its internal clients (the business unit) and top management, as they can rest assured that legal matters are handled cost-effectively and with a great sense of responsibility.

MATTER PHASES

When selecting your preferred firms and providers, ensure that they have integrated legal project management principles into their daily work. Find out how, when and for what type of projects they use project management. For example, ask the following questions:

- ☑ What technology do your firms and providers use to send standard reports to clients?
- ☑ How do your firms and providers work to continually improve their established processes?
- ☑ How have your firms and providers established project management as part of their client work?

Once you have selected your provider and have awarded the work, take the following steps:

(1) **Define**: Your provider needs to clearly understand the scope of the engagement, the parties involved, and your desired objectives and results.
- What do you, as the client, need?
- What are your expectations?
- What are your preferences in regards to communication?
- Who are your key contacts for which topics? Or is everything managed by a central project manager?

It is particularly important for your firm or provider to understand that precise planning and coordination with you will facilitate the subsequent process and management of the engagement.

Discuss all the above aspects in a joint kick-off meeting and record them in a legal matter project definition template. This document, which needs to be agreed to and signed by both parties, enables all steps to be carried out in the next phase.

(2) **Plan**: During this phase, plan all details of the legal project (including schedule, resources, risk management or communications plan). You review the initial budget and check whether the discussions about scope and deliverables have changed any assumptions that originally formed the basis for the fee proposal.

You now have a final scope of legal work and a project plan that provides you with the details of the project, including the final budget planning which also forms the basis for a corresponding budget monitoring and controlling.

Law firms have established legal project management generally to increase their efficiency and more efficiency allows for a reduction of the hourly effort. Efficiency can be achieved for example, through delegation and more diverse teams. With the aim of ensuring transparency of the status and budget spending of individual project phases, firms increasingly offer the use of digital platforms for select projects.

Depending on the type of platform, this also serves the client as a knowledge database for the provided legal advice, thus avoiding repeat legal advice on the same issue, resulting in cost savings. The higher the efficiency and productivity in the case of an agreed fixed fee, the higher the firm's profitability. Alternative pricing models therefore have an impact on performance and also meet the client's desire for budget certainty and transparency. Both proactively proposed alternative fee arrangements and the application of legal project management are an investment in a long-term relationship between client and provider.

(3) **Deliver**: Your firm or provider needs to deliver and manage the matter to your expectations in terms of costs and agreed objectives. Changes in scope, deliverables as well as issues and risks need to be managed accordingly. A legal project manager needs to compare the work done with the work originally planned considering tasks, milestones, quality standards, timeline, and budget.

Earned Value Management can be very helpful as it helps monitor a matter and evaluates whether the direction is right by comparing work done against work originally planned. It also informs you how much of the budget and time should have been spent so far.

It can also be very useful for project forecasting: For providers, tracking the costs incurred against the budget means ensuring and maintaining efficiency in their work. For the client, cost efficiency and predictability of the resulting costs are the decisive arguments for budget controlling.

A regular Matter Status Update Report by the legal project manager according to the agreed communication plan ensures that both the project team and you as the client are continuously informed about the matter. It also allows you to review the budget and incorporate it into your planning.

To manage change, use the updated matter information to track your original assumptions. Changes in the assumptions will nearly always also result in budget amendments. This also applies to situations where the scope of work has been changed and thus differs from the original scope description (for example, if you want to extend the scope of work or by any external circumstances.) Amendments must be checked and expressly agreed upon between the firm and the client. Also check the impact on planning, budget and the originally specified deliverables and incorporate those into the project plan. If the impacts and dependencies on the matter are not taken into account, this can derail the success of the project, especially with regard to efficiency, profitability, the costs, and time schedule.

Agree on rules of collaboration with your firms and providers:
- When do you have to approve a budget amendment?
- What requirements must be met for this?
- Where have you contractually agreed to this?
- Was a particular change not yet foreseeable when the original budget was released?
- How is this reflected in the assumptions?
- What will you do if the firm does not follow the agreed rules?

(4) **Close**: In the final phase of the project, the main task is to conclude and evaluate. Request a Closing Report, in which the firm compares the original objectives with the actual results:

- Are there any deviations?
- If there are, what are the reasons for it?
- What consequences result for you as the client?

Also request a final status report showing the final costs. For any topics that have an impact on the relationship between you and your provider, ask for a post-matter debrief with the entire project team. Discuss the following:

- Have your expectations as a client been met, not met, or exceeded?
- Was the originally agreed budget met?
- If the budget could not be met, what impact does it have on the supplier performance evaluation?
- What impact does the performance evaluation have on your future relationship?
- What are your "lessons learned"? How can you integrate those into future work?

CHECKLIST:

☑ Prior to the mandate: Ensure that your preferred providers have integrated legal project management principles into their work and use a structured approach for scoping. Do they offer a technical solution to ensure transparency and efficiency?

☑ Work constructively with your firm in the kick-off meeting and articulate as clearly as possible what you need, expect, and want.

☑ Express your expectations regarding communication and collaborative work with the firm on a final budget based on the knowledge gained from this phase.

☑ Ask for matter status update reports and use them for your internal budget management. Make sure that client tasks are included to avoid process delays.

☑ Check the following:
- Contract management–Are regulations on budget increases contractually agreed upon?
- Matter Management–Request a closing report
- Relationship and Performance Management– Conduct a post-matter debrief

One of the most effective ways to create value is through innovation. Innovation involves the creation, development and implementation of a new product, process and/or service, with the aim of improving efficiency, effectiveness or a competitive advantage.

Innovation must be a cornerstone of firm and provider performance, the continuous improvement of all parts of customer experience intended to reduce costs and or create competitive advantage. To get your firms and other providers to innovate, define and select innovation-related objectives you expect them to achieve within prescribed time periods. Innovation must be embedded in all discussions with your firms and providers and remain a regular feature of all performance assessments. Assessing and properly documenting the principal advantages and disadvantages associated with the selection and retention of a given vendor, on the preceding considerations, is an important task of Legal Procurement.

The following showcase examples of innovations in the legal industry:

Capability development*: To ensure continuous improvement plan with your firms and providers, start with introducing a robust assessment of their level of innovation. Record a "baseline" innovation performance score for each firm and provider. Identify and compare the performance of non-innovating firms and providers with a history of developing new products or services. Your initial assessment could include the following questions: Does the firm or provider:*

- ☑ Offer fees on a flexible schedule?
- ☑ Properly assign non-legal services to lower-cost personnel (or outsource)?
- ☑ Correctly and consistently adhere to the agreed cost structure?
- ☑ Judiciously use alternative dispute resolution?
- ☑ Understand the need to adopt key performance indicators to assess their own performance?
- ☑ Use technology appropriately?
- ☑ Produce reports created in-line with your organization's requirements?
- ☑ Offer to modify services in any way (e.g. online access to information, metrics on closed matters)?

Use of automated reports: Design and deploy automated reports in collaboration with your IT function and/or your software provider. As you develop the reports, ask the following questions:

- ☑ Do the reports provide you with the data needed to measure performance?
- ☑ Is the data reliable?
- ☑ Are you overlooking data points that are available in your systems and/or software?
- ☑ Have you engaged in a critical process to assess current internal and external needs for information?

LEGAL SPEND MANAGEMENT

Legal spend management is one of Procurement's main tasks when managing law firms and providers. You will have to find ways to manage and reduce legal spend without a negative impact on the quality of advice received or the achieved outcomes.

It is important to understand which approaches will bring the fastest results, best outcomes, and cause the least disruption (and take less convincing of your stakeholders in the legal department).

Learn about the pros and cons of different cost-savings initiatives to understand how you should prioritize and strategically approach legal spend management.

LEGAL SPEND UNDER MANAGEMENT

Legal departments traditionally took a passive management approach to legal spend: They developed and deployed policies and procedures that encourage self-regulation of spend management, but often take little direct influence on benefits and savings. Lately, a more active management approach means that the legal department (with Legal Procurement's help) actively engages with outside counsel to ensure policies and procedures are followed while benefits and savings are realized. Collaborative Management goes a step further and includes developing shared accountability between outside counsel and in-house lawyers to deliver innovative, mutually beneficial solutions.

Legal spend management initiatives range from simple process or policy changes to more complex and comprehensive programs. Each initiative can deliver cost savings for the company and offer certain performance benefits. Different initiatives also have varying time horizons and may be better suitable for certain organizations and cultures than others.

The matrix should serve as a general guide, conducting a specific mapping exercise for your organization will help you prioritize your legal spend management initiatives:

- ☑ **Time to Achieve Benefits**: Strategies in the left quadrants typically realize benefits more quickly than strategies in the right quadrants.
- ☑ **Change Management Requirements**: Strategies in the bottom quadrants tend to be easier to deploy – either technically or politically – than strategies in the top quadrants.
- ☑ **Benefit Opportunity**: Larger circles show strategies that are more likely to deliver greater cost savings than strategies indicated by smaller circles.

1	Strategic Invoice Review*
2	Strategic Matter Assignment*
3	Preferred Panel Program
4	Rates and Timekeepers*
5	Matter Budgets*
6	Legal Project Management
7	Business Reviews*
8	Alternative Sourcing/Law Companies
9	Manage Billing/ELM
10	Digital/AI

* Efficacy enhanced by ELM/Digital

LEGAL SPEND MANAGEMENT MATRIX

185

A legal department that requires fast cost control measures might select projects in the bottom-left quadrant, while an organization looking for large and sustainable benefits across a longer time horizon might consider projects in the top right quadrant.

NOTE: The numbering is not intended to imply that legal spend management initiatives should be conducted in exactly this order. When designing your strategic program, begin with both short and long-term work streams so you can realize the benefits both quickly and consistently. It is important to evaluate and understand your organization's capacity to implement the chosen initiatives, considering budgets, resource constraints, and the ability to absorb change. Typically, it makes sense to start with the areas that will gain measurable savings relatively quickly, and work your way up as demonstrable results take hold.

LEGAL INVOICE REVIEW AND BILLING GUIDELINES

Time to Achieve Benefits	Change Management	Benefit Opportunity
1-3 Months	Low	2-6 percent reduction in spend

Legal Invoice Review is the process of applying Billing Guidelines (aka Outside Counsel Billing Guidelines) to law firm invoices and adjusting invoices when they are non-compliant with the guidelines.

Billing Guidelines should provide outside counsel with your expectations regarding billing procedures. Billing Guidelines identify what tasks and expenses are compensable and which format to use for outside counsel's billing. When you develop your Billing Guidelines, focus on clarity: Your expectations and the consequences of non-compliance must be clear and unambiguous to your outside counsel.

While legal departments are regularly tasked with reviewing invoices before payment, a strategic Legal Invoice Review goes further. In a first step, a centralized invoice review team conducts the initial review, then an in-house lawyer reviews the invoice. This ensures consistency in how reviews are conducted and reduces administration time for in-house lawyers.

Some in-house counsel may be concerned that adjusting bills negatively impacts the relationship with their firms – however, a review that adheres to best practices, adjusts for clear guideline violations, and bears in mind the spirit of the invoice and the overall relationship will minimize disruption and encourage a healthy program.

A centralized invoice review team can be organized in a relatively short time – typically in less than 45 days. As part of the rollout, you should update your organization's Billing Guidelines, distribute and communicate them to all in-house staff and outside counsel via trainings, webinars, and Q&As. This helps set expectations and manage change.

Start with a "light" review before moving to stronger controls. This allows in-house lawyers to calibrate their expectations with the invoice review team. It also gives the review team time to coach outside counsel and helps facilitate the timely payment of invoices without unnecessary rejections. While cost savings are dependent on the level of review applied, a properly aligned invoice review program will save the time lawyers spend on reviewing as the invoices are properly noted to their expectations.

HOW TO MANAGE IT

Step 1:
- ☑ Update Billing Guidelines; distribute and confirm with outside counsel.
- ☑ Expense rules are defined in eBilling, some fee rules have been developed.
- ☑ Invoice review is potentially centralized, but focused on billing compliance, not error adjustments.

Step 2:
- ☑ First-level invoice review is implemented for the majority of spend.
- ☑ Optimized fee and expense rules are implemented within the eBilling platform.
- ☑ A well-defined appeals process is implemented to manage issues and disputes.

☑ Detailed reporting on law firm performance is provided to stakeholders to correct performance gaps.

Step 3:

☑ Clean and accurate invoice review data is used to inform rate negotiations and develop fixed fees.

☑ Invoice review is managed upstream by the law firm or as a shared responsibility.

Time to Achieve Benefits	Change Management	Benefit Opportunity
6-12 Months	Medium	10-20 percent reduction in spend

Strategic Matter Assignment means strategically assigning matters to specific firms to ensure the right "fit," quality, and price through a formalized, controlled, and consistent approach. This includes:

- Detailed matter scoping
- Identifying appropriate firms to approach
- Assigning matters via competitive commercial processes such as RFPs/tendering or auctions
- Negotiation processes based on clearly defined proposal details and success criteria
- Recording the engagement, its scope, commercial aspects and underlying assumptions
- Monitoring matter progress against agreed terms throughout the duration of the matter.

A supportive Legal Procurement team will find ways to adapt its traditional tools so that, potentially, each matter could be competitively scoped to ensure the correct fit.

To succeed:

☑ **Set clear expectations:** Spell out expected behaviors in your governance guidelines or policy - e.g. when to use tendering, guidance for negotiating rates or AFAs, the use of panel or off-panel firms. Actively consult both in-house counsel and outside counsel on these expectations to gain their buy-in (and compliance).

☑ **Support key expectations with dedicated resourcing, technology, and data**: If you intend to make use of tendering, provide a dedicated resource to help issue RFPs and make proposal comparisons. If you intend to encourage the use of AFAs, have a resource dedicated to scoping work, tracking successful AFAs and capture AFA-related data across your organization to support future negotiations. If the use of a panel arrangement requires convergence of the number of firms, ensure in-house counsel have ready access to panel firm competencies, negotiated rates and those value-added 'extras' which are often forgotten about during individual matter negotiations.

Technology can potentially support any process-driven activity and help track your data: e.g. look at standardizing scoping and RFP inputs/outputs such as Q&A, rates, and resourcing tables. There are many technology solutions which may help you at the selection stage. Alternatively, you may choose simple SharePoint or form-based processes.

☑ **Embrace change management aspects and track compliance, and successes**: Focus on key areas of external spend, look for champions of the new process, track both successes and failures, continually assess priorities and areas of focus, and discuss the development at leadership team meetings.

HOW TO MANAGE IT

Step 1:

- ☑ Selection and instruction policy/guidelines have been circulated and embedded with in-house and external counsel.
- ☑ Supporting data for negotiated rates, extras, and points of contact at the firm etc. are readily available for in-house counsel for use on new instructions.

Step 2:

- ☑ Dedicated resources are available to support selection and instruction activities.
- ☑ Metrics on department performance against policy expectations and formal savings are tracked.
- ☑ Regular updates and forecasts of legal matter pipeline are given to enable proactive approach to instruction support.

Step 3:

- ☑ Regular playback and 360-degree feedback of instructions and tenders with firms.
- ☑ Data sharing in key areas such as tracking against assumptions/experience of effort and resourcing against similar scopes of work.

PREFERED PANEL PROGRAM

Time to Achieve Benefits	Change Management	Benefit Opportunity
6-12 Months	High	10-40 percent reduction in spend

A preferred panel program is a purposefully-defined group of firms or providers, each covering a designated portion of the client's overall portfolio of work. Clients can gain the benefits of improved financial bargaining power from consolidation as well as closer working partnerships with firms and a reduction in administrative burden and overhead.

The ultimate goal is to have a stable of firms that view themselves as true partners and extensions of the legal department and are incented accordingly.

To develop a preferred panel, the legal department must first understand the overall portfolio of work, historical spend in key areas, firms currently used, and how they see the work being most effectively divided and/or combined.

Gather and request data from the eBilling system to detect spending patterns and opportunities for achieving economies of scale through consolidation. Once mapped out, gather input from stakeholders on how the incumbent firms are performing and define a lit of viable candidates for inclusion in the panel.

Select firms, typically via an RFP or bidding process, and provide candidate firms and providers with enough information to have a clear understanding of the nature and volume of work they wish to bid for so they can make an informed decision.

Step 1:
- ☑ Hourly rate RFPs are distributed via standard RFP tools.
- ☑ Negotiations are based on submitted rate cards and benefits calculated against negotiation results.

Step 2:
- ☑ Hourly rate RFPs are distributed to outside counsel to establish legal panels by matter type.
- ☑ Data driven RFPs are aimed to calculate average rates against historical spending and model future benefits.
- ☑ Savings are tracked and measured in detail as new matters (or existing matters) are transitioned to the panel.

Step 2:
- ☑ AFA opportunities are identified via data analysis and proposed to outside counsel.
- ☑ Sub-panel RFPs are issued to develop different panel tiers.

Preferred panel programs are only as effective as the amount of care they are given. You cannot expect to achieve the meaningful savings and reduced administrative overhead associated with the panel unless you commit to maintaining the relationships. At a minimum, this involves regular status checks, summits, and 360-degree performance reviews to ensure both sides are getting the benefit of the bargain.

While a legal panel can be an excellent cost reduction tool, it is important to note that those cost savings may not be realized for a while. Legal panel revisions may only impact new matters, which means that any historical matter – many which can last for years – may not be billed at the new rates.

Hence, benefits may only apply to a few matters early on, and gradually build as old matters close and new matters cycle in. For that reason, do not calculate the full benefit, but rather model out how savings will increase as the panel is utilized more and more, and measure more than just the old price compared to the new price, but consider benefits derived from improved staffing as well.

Additionally, there will be a sizeable portion of matters managed by firms that did not make the panel. You may need to choose between allowing non-panel firms to continue to process these "old" matters (and potentially incur additional costs or lowered service) or transitioning these matters to new firms at a substantial rework cost. In either case, the legal department will require continued support throughout the first year in order to monitor and manage the matter portfolio.

Time to Achieve Benefits	Change Management	Benefit Opportunity
1-6 Months	Medium	Approx. 5 percent reduction in spend on new timekeepers

Rate and Timekeeper Management includes active negotiation of rates/fees, managing rate increases as well as the intake and approval of new timekeepers.

The purpose of Rate and Timekeeper Management is to reduce lawyer administrative time and to separate rate conversations from the overall relationship management. By centralizing work to an invoice processing team with clearly defined roles and an objective approval system, outside counsel rates and, equally important, proper staffing can be maintained.

Rate and Timekeeper Management includes the approval of annual rate increases as well as the intake and approval of new timekeepers added to new (or existing) matters. Legal departments have historically lacked a sound method for verifying whether rates charged are within a reasonable range for the type of the work performed. Collecting, processing, and approving timekeepers and rates puts tremendous operational strain on in-house counsel. In a decentralized process, in-house counsel often either "automatically" approve rates and new timekeepers (which increases costs and risk) or conduct one-off negotiations that may add as much cost as the problem they aim to solve.

A more efficient way to manage rates and timekeepers would be to centralize rate requests, process them according to a defined set of criteria, and manage the onboarding of new timekeepers or rates to ensure entries are compliant. You could check:

- Has the timekeeper received a rate request in the past two years?
- Does the in-house lawyer agree this timekeeper is necessary for this (or future) matters?

A more elaborate approach would include in-depth analysis that considers portfolio and/or market data in evaluating a rate, such as:

- Is the timekeeper within [X] percent of the average rates within the company's portfolio of similar matters given location and level of experience?
- Is the timekeeper's requested rate within generally accepted market ranges?
- Is the timekeeper's requested rate and level prudent for the work considered, based on risk and complexity of the matter?

A data-driven process that utilizes your own portfolio data to evaluate decision conditions will provide an excellent benchmark during negotiations. There is no better benchmark than what you have historically paid to negotiate with your firms. Market or industry data can add a level of refinement to ensure that your rates are not only appropriate for your own business, but also compare well to what organizations pay.

Be careful when benchmarking your data: Check if the data from third-party sources tracks effectively paid rates or "rack" rates (non-discounted rates). Or does it show pooled billing data, which may reflect the discount/buying power of clients contributing to the pooled data (which may be dramatically different from yours)? Also check if the benchmarking data takes into account discounts outside the hourly rate (e.g. volume discounts or relationship credits). Finally, when using benchmarks, ensure that they are from organizations similar to yours in industry, size, complexity, and location.

Centralizing timekeeper-processing saves in-house counsel time and relieves them of one of their least favorite administrative tasks. The initial step can usually be done in a relatively short amount of time: as timekeeper management procedures are often included in a company's outside counsel guidelines, you may only need to re-distribute (or refresh) your guidelines. In a second step, develop your organization's "rate wizard", your criteria for objectively reviewing rates. The better your grasp of your own portfolio and rate data, the better your data model will be.

You may experience some pushback when you put in place more stringent rate management rules. This can often be solved by a clear explanation of the process, rules, and controls, and the welcome relieve of administrative time off your lawyers' plates. To mitigate concerns about negotiating on more complex or significant matters, add a step to evaluate rates with your in-house lawyers until they become more comfortable.

If your purchasing power in the market permits, move firms to a common date/time period for rate increase submissions and proactively notify firms when they are allowed to increase their rates – rather than waiting for them to come to you with their demands.

Step 1:

- ☑ Rate requests are centralized to reduce lawyer administrative time.
- ☑ The eBilling system is configured to automatically cap rates at the mutually agreed-upon price.
- ☑ Rate approvals are controlled by your organization, not the firm. This ensures correct rates are entered and only approved timekeepers are onboarded.
- ☑ Rates are confirmed as submitted, or via workflow-driven approvals.

Step2:

- ☑ Develop an approach to systematize rate reviews and uniformly apply common criteria (i.e. ensuring all rates adhere to "rate lock" policies).
- ☑ Rates are compared to portfolio billing data to ensure compliance with the legal department's own benchmarks.
- ☑ Rates may be compared to market data.

Step 3:

- ☑ Comprehensive timekeeper rates are used to inform rate negotiations and develop fair fixed fees.
- ☑ The client and firm have better discussions around the right resources to work on the right matters.

Time to Achieve Benefits	Change Management	Benefit Opportunity
6-9 Months	Medium	5-10 percent reduction in spend

The purpose of Matter Budgeting is to set clear cost expectations for each matter. You need to collect information and analyze budgets to control (previously) unknown spend at the outset of a matter, either as a competitive bid or as a single budget request.

Budgeting can range from a high-level number submitted by the primary lawyer on the matter ("top down" approach) to an in-depth budget using phases, tasks, and specific activities ("bottom up" approach). While all matters should require a budget, consider the effort to capture and track budgets:

☑ Assign a top-down budget to matters with expected spend *below* a certain threshold (as intensive management will produce diminishing returns)
☑ Require a bottom up budget to matters above a certain threshold

Budgeting can substantially impact overall legal spend. Strict adherence to budgets and overages can generate large write-offs as firms are brought into line and expectations are set. In the longer term, budgets should become more accurate. This may reduce traceable cost savings (i.e. calculating benefits based on write-offs), but results in a reduction of overall spend and cost per matter phase and task.

More than any other strategy, budgeting requires the right tools and technologies in place to measure and monitor budgets, variances, and cost savings, and firm dedication on the part of the in-house lawyers to set and hold firms accountable to the budgets.

Budgeting may include both process and analytics components. A budget intake form should be constructed and distributed to firms to complete to the level of detail established (top down or bottom up), and submitted via a centralized collection process. That data can then be aggregated into a summary or rolled up into a budget viewable by the relevant practice group. To then track actual spending compared to budget, create a data feed from the legal department's eBilling system to capture actuals and report out overages.

Although spend benefits may not be realized until much later, setting budgets will immediately help you predict and forecast future legal spend. For certain matter types or specific matters, the budget-setting process can also encourage a shift to fixed fees, which can improve legal spend.

It is important that you have executive buy-in before initiating a budgeting program. Already a challenging process, a budgeting program will be substantially harder to deploy when trying to coordinate with unsupportive team members. Start with certain matter types, geographies, or deploy a tiered budget program that focuses on significant matters only.

Step 1:

- ☑ A centralized budget program is deployed to capture estimated quarterly or annual spend by matter (usually "top down" budgeting).
- ☑ Budgets are tied to an "actuals" report using data in an eBilling system and/or accounts payable.
- ☑ May include budgeting flags when total amounts approach a certain threshold (i.e. 75 percent of a matter).

Step 2:

- ☑ Establish clear expectation that budgets should not be exceeded. Instead, they are either proactively re-forecasted due to extreme events, capped or written off.
- ☑ High spend matters are managed using "bottom up" budgeting.
- ☑ Budget reviews are incorporated into quarterly business reviews.

Step 3:

- ☑ "Bottom up" budgeting is used for a larger portion of matters.
- ☑ Additional technologies are used to track Work in Progress. Invoicing and project status information may be used on a continuous basis.
- ☑ Budget management reports on the reasons for budget changes, not only that a budget change has occurred.

LEGAL PROJECT MANAGEMENT

Time to Achieve Benefits	Change Management	Benefit Opportunity
6-9 Months	High	5-10 percent reduction in spend

Legal Project Management involves employing a disciplined approach to planning how a matter will be handled as well as continuous monitoring and course-correction during the life of the matter. The benefits of Legal Project Management include tighter alignment of expectations, improved outcomes, fewer financial surprises (for both clients and firms), and lower overall costs.

HOW TO MANAGE IT

Step 1:
Clearly define and document the scope of work, including:
- ☑ Project execution plans (steps, stages, sequences, and expected timing)
- ☑ Staffing and roles/responsibilities
- ☑ Expected costs/budgets

Step 2:
- ☑ Scenario modeling ("if this, then that") and change management
- ☑ Communication protocols
- ☑ Document management

Step 3:
- ☑ Follow up on the plan, work closely to monitor progress through regular status meetings and reporting. It is often beneficial to employ dedicated Project Management professionals to run a matter or portfolio of matters to gain the greatest effectiveness.

Time to Achieve Benefits	Change Management	Benefit Opportunity
3-?? Months	Low (to High)	0-?? percent reduction in spend

Business reviews are an important part of proactive law firm management, as they help set expectations and facilitate developing a mutually beneficial relationship. While the content of a business review depends on the maturity of the relationship with the firm, a full review includes:

- ☑ A **quantitative review** to analyze spend trends and cost variances.
- ☑ Once clear spending expectations have been set, the focus can shift to include a **qualitative review**, measuring performance against company-defined goals or service levels.
- ☑ A mature 360-degree relationship will include a **collaborative review** with shared goals, aimed to identify or track progress on common initiatives.

Your business review should focus on driving results. Any data presented should tell a story and drive the participant to a decision, by identifying wins, communicating gaps and resolutions, or moving forward towards a mutual goal.

To be scalable, develop a template to uniformly collect business review metrics. This can be as simple as a PowerPoint slide or as robust as a business intelligence-supported dashboard.

The act of scheduling and hosting business reviews can be time consuming, even with standardized templates. Give the purpose of the review a fair amount of thought before you dedicate significant time to the business reviews.

Organize them based on relationship size and criticality:

- For **smaller relationships**, distribute business review reports with action items.
- For **larger relationships**, host periodic reviews (semi-annually or annually).
- For **premium relationships**, host quarterly reviews.

Start with a pilot review to develop and refine your template and a cadence that works for your organization before rolling out a full-scale program.

As a cost savings measure, business reviews can be used to request credits, negotiate rates and drive performance improvement, but the real value in these programs is to serve as a forum for collaboration where innovations are discussed and significant impacts are measured.

Business reviews are typically easy to initiate since law firms love to meet their clients, but can become more challenging as the focus moves from informing outside counsel about new initiatives to requiring them to meet goals or change their behavior. It is important to build on each subsequent review so that change happens consistently.

A mature relationship may separate the tactical billing and service level agreement (SLA) measurement discussions from the innovative reviews so the meetings can focus on strategic projects rather than billing issues. If the relationship is healthy, any issues can be resolved without lawyer involvement.

HOW TO MANAGE IT

Step 1:
- ☑ Spend metrics and qualitative measurements shared with firms.
- ☑ Firm is provided ranking information against its portfolio peers.
- ☑ Firm may provide its (own) performance data.

Step 2:
- ☑ Data exchanged includes scores, targets, SMART goals, and SMART recommendations (Specific, Measurable, Attainable, Relevant, and Time-bound).
- ☑ Possible penalties or rewards are devised and communicated during meetings.
- ☑ Firm is expected to provide metrics to support a full 360 degree-scorecard review.

Step 3:
- ☑ Tactical reviews are discussed in separate meetings or are immaterial due to alternative billing structures.
- ☑ Metrics focus increasingly on innovations and best practices.
- ☑ Business reviews can include legal project management reviews.

Time to Achieve Benefits	Change Management	Benefit Opportunity
1-18 (or more) Months	Low to High	20-80 percent reduction in spend on specific areas alternatively sourced

Alternative Sourcing is intended to optimize the allocation of legal resources by engaging third-parties (that are not law firms) for distinct legal tasks that can be separated and completed individually.

Assess tasks for:

- ☑ **Complexity**: What are the skills and experience level needed to complete the task?
- ☑ **Volume**: Is the task repeatable and does it repeat often enough to justify engaging additional resources?
- ☑ **Prioritization**: Which factors can impact the success of engaging alternate sourcing, such as required turnaround, visibility, importance, and level of risk?

Once you identified and assessed discrete tasks, a process flow can be built around the tasks to coordinate work between in-house counsel and third-party resources.

Alternative Sourcing aims to reduce cost and turnaround times for legal services by utilizing third-party legal resources instead of in-house resources or traditional outside counsel.

Some of the most cost-effective and beneficial solutions include:

- ☑ Contracts lifecycle management (including development of templates, playbooks, processes and protocols)
- ☑ Contracts gathering, analysis, migration, and storage
- ☑ Contract review, negotiation, and execution
- ☑ Discovery support and document review
- ☑ Event monitoring and data breach remediation
- ☑ Due diligence for mergers and acquisitions
- ☑ Substantive legal advice and counsel (when appropriately structured for compliance with regulations governing the practice of law)
- ☑ Legal staff augmentation

HOW TO MANAGE IT

Step 1:
- ☑ Identify alternative sourcing opportunity
- ☑ Unbundle
- ☑ Prioritize strategic objectives

Step 2:
- ☑ Choose management strategy
- ☑ Right source
- ☑ Sourcing design

Step 3:
- ☑ Create infrastructure
- ☑ Change management
- ☑ Implement alternate sourcing

Weigh the potential benefits alongside strategic objectives:
- Cost reduction/savings
- Freeing time for internal resources and/or reducing use of outside counsel
- Compliance risk/mitigation
- Decreasing turnaround times

Active management of alternate sourcing with limited engagement of other business departments or third parties can be accomplished with very little change management. When other business departments or third parties will be impacted and the engagement is extensive, executive sponsorship and carefully planned and executed change management are critical to successful implementation.

Time to Achieve Benefits	Change Management	Benefit Opportunity
6-18 Months	Medium	5-15 percent reduction in spend and efficiencies

Legal software tools, once known as "matter management" and "electronic billing" have evolved into sophisticated suites of products now referred as "Enterprise Legal Management." They provide additional benefits such as sophisticated workflow management and enhanced data-capture and organizational techniques. These tools remain indispensable for streamlining the legal department's work as well as the intake, review, approval, and payment of legal invoices.

Reporting has also become increasingly sophisticated. Where once legal departments could mainly only track actual spending, new systems now allow detailed KPI, metrics, and data-visualization tools.

To select the right system gather detailed use requirements, conduct a selection exercise, and be clear about growth plans and changing priorities in the future to ensure you make an investment that can grow with you.

DIGITAL/ARTIFICIAL INTELLIGENCE

Digital/Artificial Intelligence refers to the newest generation of technology that goes beyond storing and moving data to gain insights hidden in the data itself. From a legal spend management perspective, this offer legal departments the ability to mine their own large volumes of historical spend data, invoice details, and matter details to find opportunities for savings that were not previously obvious.

AI tends to work best when there are fairly large groups of similar matters to study and learn from, to help the machines "learn" over time.

KEY PERFORMANCE INDICATORS AND HEAT MAPS

It is best practice to regularly assess the performance of law firms and other legal services using Key Performance Indicators (KPIs). This allows them to demonstrate and showcase their strengths and the benefits of hiring a particular firm over its competitors.

Please note: Alternative legal services providers and legal process outsourcing companies can cover a multitude of legal support services such as eDiscovery or eDisclosure, document review, other legal process outsourcing processes including non-disclosure agreement (NDA) negotiations, procurement contract negotiations etc. and legal technology. Many of the KPIs presented can be used for these services as well.

KPI FOR FIRMS AND PROVIDERS

To assess the quality of the relationship with the firm or provider, use online surveys and measure the following KPI:
- ☑ Level of Collaboration
- ☑ Level of Transparency
- ☑ Level of Compatibility
- ☑ Level of Innovation

To assess the firm or provider's (general) performance, use online surveys and measure the following KPI:
- ☑ Quality of advice
- ☑ Timeliness of advice
- ☑ Commerciality of advice/(legal) strategy
- ☑ Understanding of business requirements
- ☑ Flexibility in approach
- ☑ Value for money (define meaning in your organization)
- ☑ Percentage of AFAs vs. Hourly Rate
- ☑ Value-added services (e.g. secondees, rebates etc.)

To assess the firm or provider's level of compliance with your organization's requirements, use your eBilling system and work with your legal invoice/bill review team or provider and measure the following KPI:
- ☑ Policy compliance
- ☑ Budget compliance
- ☑ Outside counsel guidelines compliance
- ☑ Rate compliance
- ☑ AFA compliance

To assess the firm or provider's timekeeper management, use your eBilling system and work with your legal invoice/bill review team or provider and measure the following KPI:
- ☑ Timekeeper total spend
- ☑ Timekeeper utilization
- ☑ Timekeeper location
- ☑ Timekeeper diversity statistics
- ☑ Timekeeper activity appropriateness

Note: It is also best practice to ask your law firms and legal services providers to give you a 360-degree performance feedback to help drive overall performance improvements.

To assess matters: It is best practice to measure matters on the following KPI:

- ☑ Total spend on the matter
- ☑ Average blended rates of the professionals working on your matter(s)
- ☑ Matter duration
- ☑ Average years of experience per partner working on your matter(s)
- ☑ Phase length of the matter

To assess firms/providers: It is best practice to measure firms and providers on the following KPI:

- ☑ Total spend with the firm/provider
- ☑ Satisfaction rating with the firm/provider
- ☑ Volume of active matters with the firm/provider
- ☑ Average blended rate of the firm's/provider's professionals working for you
- ☑ Matter cost vs. benchmark
- ☑ Matter duration vs. benchmark
- ☑ Timekeepers per matter
- ☑ Average years of experience per partner working for you

When reviewing invoices, look for red flags. Some signs can be indicative of a larger problem.

To identify excessive billing, check the following:
- ☑ Timekeepers billed out over [x] dollars/euros/pounds per year/per timekeeper?
- ☑ Timekeepers by hours billed: Are timekeepers billed out over 2,080 hours/year or 40 hours/week? This could be an indication of work that should be shifted in-house.
- ☑ Timekeepers frequently billed out at 12+ hours/day could indicate overworked timekeepers.
- ☑ Timekeepers billing over 20 percent of time on weekends and evenings could indicate that matters are not well managed.

To identify potential staffing issues, check the following:
- ☑ Are junior associates/newly qualified lawyers billing more than 10 percent of hours on your matters?
- ☑ Are partners tasked with clerical tasks?
- ☑ Do firms conduct "drive-by billing", that is, many timekeepers have marginal input and bill short increments adding up to over 10 percent of total hours?

To identify billing practice issues, check the following:
- ☑ Do invoices lag 60+ days?
- ☑ Are billing codes missing on 10+ percent of line items?
- ☑ Does the firm use block billing (that is assigning a one-time charge to multiple tasks) to 10+ percent on the firm level or 25+ percent on the timekeeper level?

Feedback Template

These Feedback questions/statement are designed to capture current perceptions of the Panel Firm relationship. Please review each question/statement and provide your comments to support any 'Very Strong' scores to support the statement. Give your assessment of the current state against each question/statement by selecting the number that corresponds to the evidence you believe exists: **1 = Strongly Disagree; 2 = Disagree; 3 = Neutral; 4 = Agree; 5 = Strongly Agree.**

LOB PLEASE ENSURE THIS FIELD IS COMPLETED				

Relationship	#	Statements	Score (1-5)	Comments
Commitment	1	We are fully committed to our relationship		
Working together	2	We have a good and effective working relationship		
Transparency	3	We are transparent and honest in all our dealings		
	4	We provide accurate and reasonable invoices		
Compatibility	5	We are user friendly for the Claims Teams		
	6	We deal with any issue in a timely fashion		
Innovation	7	We share our innovations and improvement plans		
	8	We are proactive in sharing our Business strategy		
Performance				
Level of Lawyer	9	We always use the appropriate level of Lawyer		
Performance	10	We have high performance standards		
	11	We work quickly to rectify any performance problems.		
Organisation	12	Our decision making process is clear and decisions are provided to client in an efficient and timely manner.		
Commercial	13	We are commercial in our advice		
	14	Our advice always reflects the balance between commerciality and legal position		
	15	We are value for money		
Quality	16	We always understand instructions received		
	17	The quality of advice we provide is of a high and detailed standard		
	18	We provide and update efficiently any budget/reserves/claims amounts		

SAMPLE TEMPLATE TO ASSESS PROVIDER PERFORMANCE AND RELATIONSHIP

These Feedback questions/statement are designed to capture current perceptions of the Panel Firm relationship. Please review each question/statement and provide your comments to support any 'Very Strong' scores to support the statement. Give your assessment of the current state against each question/statement by selecting the number that corresponds to the evidence you believe exists: **1 = Strongly Disagree; 2 = Disagree; 3 = Neutral; 4 = Agree; 5 = Strongly Agree.**

PLEASE ENSURE THIS FIELD IS COMPLETED				

Relationship	#	Statements	Score (1-5)	Comments/ Notable Handlers
Commitment	1	The client is fully committed to our relationship		
Working together	2	The client is proactive in promoting an effective relationship		
Transparency	3	They are transparent and honest		
	4	They challenges our invoices		
	5	Invoices challenges are reasonable		
Compatibility	6	They are approachable		
	7	They deal with issues in a timely fashion		
Innovation	8	They share their innovations and improvement plans with us		
	9	They are active with sharing their business strategy with us		
Performance				
Level of Lawyer	10	They will challenge/question where appropriate the Level of Lawyer used		
Performance	11	The handler provides an experienced level of input		
	12	They work quickly to rectify any performance problems.		
Organisation	13	Their decision making process is clear and decisions are provided to the Firm in an efficient and timely manner.		
Commercial	14	The Claims Teams have a strong claims handling strategy for each claim		
	15	The Claims Teams are clear in their settlement strategy		
Quality	16	They will challenge/question where appropriate the advice provided		
	17	They update efficiently any budget/reserves/claims amounts		

SAMPLE FEEDBACK TEMPLATE TO ASSESS CLIENT'S PERFORMANCE

The data you collect in a 360-degree review enables you to produce a heat map which assesses not only your relationships, but also shows where your and the provider's opinions on performance diverge. When meeting with your providers, focus both on what works well and where your organization view greatly differs from the provider's. Your providers will need this information to be able to improve on their services and service delivery.

The heat map (see example below) illustrates the percentage value score by both client and provider: Indicate the bottom three attributes in red (or a different color of your choice); indicate the top three attributes in green (or a different color of your choice).

In the column on the right, differences or gaps in perception are marked with colored flags. A green flag indicates a gap of less than 10 percent. A yellow flag indicates a gap of 10 to 19 percent. A red flag indicates a gap of more than 20 percent.

Relationship Component	How Law Firm scores Client	How Client scores Themselves	% difference	
Commitment	60%	80%	▶	20%
Working Together	60%	77%	▷	17%
Transparency	60%	75%	▷	15%
Compatibility	80%	83%	▷	3%
Innovation	40%	67%	▶	27%
Performance Component	How Law Firm scores Client	How Client scores Themselves	% difference	
Level of Lawyer	80%	77%	▷	3%
Performance	90%	75%	▷	15%
Organisation	60%	83%	▶	23%
Commercial	70%	80%	▷	10%
Quality	80%	82%	▷	2%
Average scores	68%	78%		14%

	Law Firm	Client
Relationship & Performance total (out of 85 / 80)	58.00	62.00

SAMPLE HEAT MAP

The table below illustrates percentage values of survey respondents against each score 1-5.

Indicate the top ratings with green buttons and highlight areas of concern in red: where the percentage surpasses a threshold of 10 percent for score 1 and 20 percent for score 2.

Trust Component	Law Firm				
	1	2	3	4	5
Commitment	0%	0%	100%	0%	0%
Working Together	0%	0%	100%	0%	0%
Transparency	0%	50%	0%	50%	0%
Compatibility	0%	0%	0%	100%	0%
Innovation	0%	100%	0%	0%	0%

Control Component	Law Firm				
	1	2	3	4	5
Level of Lawyer	0%	0%	0%	100%	0%
Performance	0%	0%	0%	50%	50%
Organisation	0%	0%	100%	0%	0%
Commercial	0%	0%	0%	50%	0%
Quality	0%	0%	0%	100%	0%

Trust Component	Client				
	1	2	3	4	5
Commitment	0%	0%	0%	100%	0%
Working Together	0%	0%	17%	83%	0%
Transparency	8%	0%	8%	75%	8%
Compatibility	0%	0%	0%	83%	17%
Innovation	0%	0%	67%	33%	0%

Control Component	Client				
	1	2	3	4	5
Level of Lawyer	0%	0%	17%	83%	0%
Performance	0%	0%	33%	58%	8%
Organisation	0%	0%	0%	83%	17%
Commercial	0%	0%	0%	100%	0%
Quality	0%	0%	0%	92%	8%

SAMPLE SCORES

To assess effectiveness of communication:
- ☑ Create templates of effective communication that become standard for all firms or providers to adopt.
- ☑ An example might be a white paper warning of impending regulatory change that, implemented early, saved a client time and cost.
- ☑ Another example might be letters of advice that proved to pay-off by being followed and positive results being achieved.

To assess information exchange:
- ☑ Create templates and measure the use of consistently applied information exchange.
- ☑ This could be monthly reports, billing information, horizon planning, team updates etc. This measure is about ensuring that your firms and providers understand your organization and make the right effort to supply and request the right level of information to enhance the relationship and make working together more than the sums of its parts.

To assess information quality:
- ☑ Establish clear guidelines on the quality of the information provided by firms and providers.
- ☑ Measure if they are followed. This must be followed and managed by all, and include the quality of the information provided to firms and providers as well as from them. Bills that do not detail task level data etc. will be reflected on the scorecard.

To assess timeliness:

☑ Agree on a clear table of expectations with firms and providers at the start of any program. When do you need a quote? And how long should it take to get it? When do you agree to pay an invoice? And what are the terms? If you leave a message and require a call back – how long should you have to wait?

☑ Map all of the areas where time is important and measure them, reporting the detail in your scorecard.

To assess level of feedback from the supplier:

☑ Regular feedback from firms and providers is a good way to understand how to adjust relationships and contracts to ensure that you provide many opportunities for your firms and providers to deliver the value you wanted from them in the first place.

☑ Do not just ask one person – get feedback from everyone who works with the firms and providers – from finance to operations, from junior-level to senior-level. This way you will quickly see how engaged the firm or provider is in ensuring they bring the best to your relationship.

To assess innovation:

☑ Incentivize firms and providers to innovate and measure them accordingly. This will make a significant difference to the value created for your organization.

☑ Listen to their ideas and adopt the best ones. You are paying them to be the best in their field, so benefit from their knowledge. Your firms and providers should produce major service innovations, process evolutions or some of significant market advantage for you. Do not use firms and providers who do not innovate.

To assess systems and technology, such as in the context of eDiscovery or eDisclosure and document review, the following are useful and best practice KPI:

Measure committed uptime (expected availability) per month or per quarter. Most clients expect a 99 percent minimum uptime. Should the technology's uptime be lower than 99 percent, clients typically expect a discount. The percentage discounts, percentage of uptime brackets and approach to calculating vary by organization, as do the mechanics around claiming discounts.

NOTE: Percentages are illustrative!

Platform Availability Percentage	Discount
99.98%+	0%
99.7 - 99.97%	1%
99.6 - 99.69%	2.50%
99.5 - 99.59%	5%
99.4 - 99.49	7.5%
99.3 - 99.39	10%
99.2 - 99.29	12%
99.1 - 99.19	15%
99 - 99.09	17.5%
98 - 98.99	20%
96 - 97.99	25%

Measure staff on-boarding: On-boarding staff is often a critical issue for clients when using alternative legal services providers.

NOTE: Numbers are illustrative!

Number of Resources (following client request)	Time to On-Board Resources
0-20	24 Hours
20-40	48 Hours
41-75	72 hours
75-100	96 Hours
100+	120 Hours

Measure issue resolution/escalation: How quickly a provider addresses and resolves a raised issue is always important, but can be particularly so in regulatory investigations and litigation where alternative legal services providers often perform work.

KPI Classification	KPI Description	Issue KPI
Severity 1 - Critical	Critical Issue: Material issue impacting client's ability to perform critical services / impacting client's litigation or regulatory investigation plans and/or strategy .	1 - 2 hours
Severity 2 - Urgent	High Importance Issue: Client is severely inconvenienced by issue although can still work	Same Business Day
Severity 4 - Service Request	General requests for information / support / MI	Next Business Day

SAMPLE KPI TO CAPTURE ISSUE
RESOLUTION/ESCALATION

Measure project management: Alternative legal services providers typically use project management extensively and should therefore be measured as well. This is particularly useful as part of a 360 degree process when the client also has an internal project manager (e.g. when working with large litigation/ regulatory investigation projects).

KPI	Project Manager 1	Project Manager 1	Project Manager 1
	1 = Excellent; 2 = Good; 3 = Poor; 4 = Very Poor	1 = Excellent; 2 = Good; 3 = Poor; 4 = Very Poor	1 = Excellent; 2 = Good; 3 = Poor; 4 = Very Poor
Responsiveness	[ENTER SCORE]	[ENTER SCORE]	[ENTER SCORE]
Communicates requirements effectively	[ENTER SCORE]	[ENTER SCORE]	[ENTER SCORE]
Team Management	[ENTER SCORE]	[ENTER SCORE]	[ENTER SCORE]
Ability to keep project on track	[ENTER SCORE]	[ENTER SCORE]	[ENTER SCORE]
Deal with issues	[ENTER SCORE]	[ENTER SCORE]	[ENTER SCORE]
Keeping documentation up to date	[ENTER SCORE]	[ENTER SCORE]	[ENTER SCORE]
Managing senior stakeholders	[ENTER SCORE]	[ENTER SCORE]	[ENTER SCORE]
Engagement with relevant parties	[ENTER SCORE]	[ENTER SCORE]	[ENTER SCORE]

SAMPLE KPI FOR PROJECT MANAGEMENT

Measure quality control/error rate: It is best practice to measure quality in terms of adherence to agreed processes as well as the quality of the provider's work product. One of the KPI is 'Error rate' on document level, project level and individual reviewer level (e.g. for document review work). Clients usually classify errors as "critical" vs. "non-critical." An example for "critical" error would be missing a privilege tag, for "non-critical" e.g. document classification.

OTHER USEFUL TOOLS

CHECKLIST CUTTING COST AND ADDING VALUE

Request value
Ask your firms/providers: How can they be more effective, streamlined, efficient, and add more value?

- ☑ Focus on process and communication, no talk of rates
- ☑ Invite recommendations about how your department operates
- ☑ Limit size and response times

Identify and avoid self-inflicted costs
Legal departments' own informal systems and processes can cause duplication and unnecessary work.

- ☑ Track how many people are part of the communication loop
- ☑ Find out what informal processes and procedures are causing extra work for you and your firms/providers
- ☑ Use metrics to track law firm performance

Consolidate
Outside counsel management time is one of the largest hidden legal costs. The average client uses too many firms/providers, each with their own informal management needs.

- ☑ Give more work to fewer firms and consider using one law firm to manage others if needed

Adopt time-based metrics

What gets measured gets done. Metrics drive behavior. Behavior drives time consumption. Work with your firms/providers to measure the right metrics. Time equals expense.

- ☑ Adopt an "estimate-to-complete" for large matters; allocate time needed to complete an assignment based on current facts and circumstances
- ☑ Adopt time-based metrics to drive new (desired) behaviors and lower costs to do business (e.g. Elapsed time to complete, Time to interim deadlines)
- ☑ Use these estimates to develop standards moving forward

Ask for fixed fees

Fixed fees, or fixed fees by phase are the most popular fee arrangements. They offer predictability and improved strategy.

- ☑ Work with your firms and providers and provide them with the data they need to triage and properly assess your work in order to give you correct estimates.
- ☑ Do not ask for shadow billing. Success demands high trust. If you don't trust the firms/providers, you should not work with them in the first place.

CHECKLIST IMPROVING LAW FIRM PERFORMANCE

Use this checklist to help ensure that your legal services providers are delivering value and bringing innovation to service delivery. No matter which enterprise legal management solution or e-billing platform you use, you can leverage the data you are already collecting and put it to work in support of improved outcomes, greater savings, and better overall business performance.

☑ **Identify your goals as an organization**: Decide on your goals and communicate them to outside counsel. Let them know which metrics you will put in place. Knowing how you plan to score them – and compare them to your other firms – will help them focus on the right areas.

☑ **Develop basic KPIs to compare firms**: Think about which KPIs best indicate your progress toward your goals. E.g.:
  • Amount of work/matters with each firm
  • Amount of spend with each firm
  • Firm results (which firms generate the best outcomes?)

☑ **Establish targeted KPIs to measure progress on specific goals**: Collect data based on your specific goals and priorities.
  • CONTROL COST: KPIs around budgeting and comparing how well firms are adhering to them. Measure how consistently firms are providing early case assessments and communicating potential red flags, as well as complying with your billing guidelines.

- IMPROVE OUTCOMES: Measure staffing ratios to ensure the right level of involvement of partners and more experienced attorneys.

☑ **Create fields to capture the necessary data**: Work with your vendor to ensure your enterprise legal management solution captures the right data. This may be a combination of fields the tool already tracks and custom fields to meet your specific needs

☑ **Design reports and scorecards that convey the information**: Communicate! Present your data so your audience can quickly find it and easily understand it. If you have multiple audiences, design multiple dashboards so that everyone gets the information they need with no extraneous data. (For example, senior managers typically want high-level information, while claims managers or in-house counsel who directly manage individual legal matters need more granular data to support their daily decisions.)

☑ **Work with your internal team to understand the drivers**: Make sure everyone is working with the same expectations and priorities so the team can be consistent on decisions about case assignments as well as the feedback they provide on firms. Survey your people for qualitative data, which is an important part of a complex analysis. Feedback forms, normally filled out by internal team members when cases are closed, can help identify law firm strengths and opportunities for improvement.

☑ **Know your go-to law firm partners**: Keep a list of firms (by practice area and geography) that consistently deliver the service and outcomes you expect, especially on complex or high-risk matters.

☑ **Regularly share your data with your firms**: Share your feedback at least once a year, including the firm's scorecard. Rather than being adversarial, this process can greatly improve your relationship with your firms. Think of it like going over your blood work at the doctor's office. It is an opportunity to see what is going well and to identify areas for improvement.

☑ **Set clear expectations about the metrics you want firms to provide**: Ask your firms to provide a spreadsheet of all the files they received from your organization in a given year. For each case, the spreadsheet must show the date of their first call with your organization and whether it was resolved or not, along with other information that helps keep the focus on strategy and ensuring that there is a game plan for each file.

BIOGRAPHIES

Haley Crain Carter

Haley is a strategic sourcing and Six Sigma expert with experience in operations, procurement, and contract management. A graduate of the Naval Academy, she worked as a logistics officer in the U.S. Marine Corps, making two combat deployments in support of Operation Iraqi Freedom. Since leaving Active Duty, Haley has led sourcing in the electronics manufacturing, chemicals distribution, and oil and gas industries. Haley earned an MBA with Distinction from the University of Liverpool and currently attends the University of Houston Law Center. She was awarded the Defense Meritorious Service Medal and the Navy and Marine Corps Commendation Medal.

Haley, Stephanie Corey, and Sue Krasaway authored "Negotiate Price" and "Negotiate Terms and Conditions."

LinkedIn: www.linkedin.com/in/haleycraincarter
Twitter: @H_C_Carter

Pamela Cone, ISSP-SA

Pamela is the founder and CEO of Amity Advisory. She provides strategic counsel to leaders of law firms around the globe to ensure the evolution of their "random acts of kindness" into strategic, transformative Social Impact and Sustainability programs that differentiate. She has more than 30 years' experience in professional services, and earned a graduate degree in Communications Management and another in Social Impact and Sustainability. She leads the Buying Legal® Council Working Group Social Impact and Sustainability.

Pamela authored the section on Social Impact and Sustainability in "Your Choices Make an Impact: Social Impact and Sustainability/Diversity & Inclusion."

LinkedIn: www.linkedin.com/in/pamelacone/
Twitter: @pamelacone
Website: www.amityadvisory.com

Stephanie Corey

Stephanie is Co-Founder & General Partner of UpLevel Ops, LLC, a legal strategy and operations consulting firm. A veteran in the Legal Operations field, Stephanie Corey began her career at Hewlett Packard Company as Chief of Staff and Head of Legal Operations. Stephanie has held similar positions at VMWare and Flex International. She is the co-founder of the Corporate Legal Operations Consortium (CLOC), a leading Legal Operations association. Stephanie holds a BA in Economics and an MBA from Lehigh University, and is a serial entrepreneur in her spare time.

Stephanie, Haley Crain Carter, and Sue Krasaway authored "Negotiate Price" and "Negotiate Terms and Conditions."

LinkedIn: www.linkedin.com/in/stephcorey-ulo/ and www.linkedin.com/company/uplevel-ops
Twitter: @StephanieACorey
Website: www.UpLevelOps.com

Dr. Orazio Difruscolo

Orazio leads Claims & Legal Sourcing at Swiss Re Group, globally. He holds a PhD in Management and has work experience in six countries, building partnerships with clients, colleagues and providers to increase revenues, reduce costs and mitigate risks. In the last decade he committed to the legal space with the ambition to create new value, elevating sourcing beyond the traditional procurement levers, working collaboratively with in-house counsel and legal services providers. Recent track records include the application of Augmented Intelligence (combining human and artificial intelligence), product development and winning new business as part of cross-functional teams. He is a Board Member of the Buying Legal® Council.

Orazio was the chapter lead for "Design a Sourcing Strategy."

LinkedIn: www.linkedin.com/in/odifruscolo/

Sandy Duncan

Sandy is Senior Sourcing Manager at Lloyds Banking Group. He is an experienced Purchasing & Supply Chain professional who joined Lloyds Banking Group in 2012 and took on the lead Legal Services Sourcing role in 2014. He has had a number of senior management positions in supply chain assessment and accreditation organizations, including being responsible for business and product development. Prior to this he was Director of Group Purchasing at Bradford & Bingley Plc. He started his career as a Print Production Manager. Sandy is a Fellow of the Chartered Institute of Procurement & Supply and served as a Board Member of the Buying Legal® Council.

Sandy authored several parts of the Guide, including "Get ready for Buying Legal Services."

LinkedIn: www.linkedin.com/in/sandyd1
Twitter: @sandyduncan1

Adrienne Fox

Adrienne is the Director of Global Category Management for Legal Services at Novartis Services Inc. As a strategic business partner, Adrienne's role focuses on delivering drive process improvements and value for law firm engagements. In addition to 20 years of procurement experience, Adrienne worked as a paralegal and compliance manager. She holds a BS in Administration of Justice & English from Rutgers College, an ABA approved Paralegal Certificate and an MA in Corporate & Organizational Communications from Farleigh Dickinson University, NJ. She is passionate about continuous learning, diversity & inclusion and her work as co-leader of the Buying Legal® Council Working Group Diversity & Inclusion.

Adrienne authored the section on Diversity & Inclusion in "Your Choices Make an Impact: Social Impact and Sustainability/Diversity & Inclusion."

LinkedIn: www.linkedin.com/in/adrienne-fox-0610299/

Steph Hogg

Steph is the Director of Validatum's® procurement consultancy services, working exclusively with law firms to optimize external legal procurement and client relationships. Bringing thought leadership to legal procurement, she is a seasoned professional with unrivalled practical experience in running legal panel processes and developing and maintaining successful, collaborative relationships. She splits her time between partner procurement and negotiation training, bid and pitch support and client tender and retention strategy consultancy. She works extensively on both private and public sector tenders and is expert at understanding the not so obvious nuances that can help law firm pitches stand out.

Steph authored "Identify the right firms and providers" and "Requests for proposal."

LinkedIn: https://www.linkedin.com/in/steph-hogg-17859a4a/
Twitter: @StephHogg1
Website: www.validatum.com

Kelly Hotchkiss

Kelly has over 20 years' experience in the insurance industry with a particular focus on the claims arena. She started her career handling claims for a global law firm and for the past 12 years has specialized in commercial insurance and reinsurance claims supplier selection and management, both at a European and international level. She has a keen interest in claims strategy, operations and spend management, focusing on how to deliver best value for money throughout the entire claims' lifecycle.

Kelly authored "Meet Stake Holder Expectations" and co-authored the chapter "Design a Sourcing Strategy."

LinkedIn: www.linkedin.com/in/kelly-hotchkiss-acii-mcips-4a40a72a/

Anja Jähnel

Anja is a Legal Procurement Professional, Legal Project Associate (IILPM) and Change Manager. Topics like legal project management and transparent pricing are close to her heart. From 2012 to 2018 she worked as Global Sourcer and Category Manager in Global Legal Spend Management and Legal Procurement at Bayer AG. Her interest in looking at the legal market from a different perspective motivated her to dive into the world of legal practice. She is now a Business Development Manager at Osborne Clarke focusing on Life Science & Healthcare and responsible for the entire bidding process for Osborne Clarke in Germany. She served as a Board Member of the Buying Legal® Council.

Anja authored "Supplier Relationship Management" and "Legal Project Management and Budget Management."

LinkedIn: www.linkedin.com/in/anja-j%C3%A4hnel-566346104/

Susan Krasaway

Susan is a Consultant at UpLevel Ops. She has a breadth of experience as a Legal Operations researcher, analyst, and author. Her works include articles and whitepapers on Legal Department change management, legal process and tech roadmaps, and the future of the legal industry. She also plays a critical role in client work, operations, and marketing. Prior to joining UpLevel, Sue worked as a television news producer, in township government administration, and writing for local newspapers. Susan holds an MA in Communication from the University of Wisconsin Superior and a BA in Psychology from Colorado College.

Sue, Haley Crain Carter, and Stephanie Corey authored "Negotiate Price" and "Negotiate Terms and Conditions."

Tina Ksienzyk

Tina is a Business Psychologist and Procurement Professional at Bayer AG with more than 9 years of experience in various spend categories and procurement projects. After working as a procurement consultant, she joined the Legal Procurement Team as global Category Lead. Over the last couple of years she drove the implementation of legal spend management and transformation of the legal category at Bayer across the globe. She served as a Board Member of the Buying Legal® Council.

Tina authored "Performance Management."

LinkedIn: www.linkedin.com/in/tina-ksienzyk-37801377/

Caroline O'Grady

Caroline is a qualified UK Solicitor and PRINCE II project management practitioner with an extensive background in law firm relationship and legal spend management. Since co-founding Coote O'Grady, Caroline has worked to build a bespoke services package specific to the European market, while still servicing global clients in all areas of legal spend. Her focus in recent years has been the development of proprietary legal technology, bringing her knowledge of the market into the tech she designs. Before developing legal technology for Coote O'Grady, Caroline helped to design and implement various legal tech products for global organizations.

Caroline and Lynsey Wood authored "Key Performance Indicators and Heat Maps."

LinkedIn: https://www.linkedin.com/in/carolineogrady1/ and www.linkedin.com/company/coote-o'grady/
Twitter: @CooteOGrady
Website: www.cooteogrady.com

Dr. Silvia Hodges Silverstein

Silvia is CEO of the Buying Legal® Council and adjunct faculty at Columbia Law School. She co-authored the Harvard Business School case studies GlaxoSmithKline: Sourcing Complex Professional Services on the company's legal procurement initiative and Riverview Law: Applying Business Sense to the Legal Market on the new model law firm. Silvia also wrote articles for *The Georgetown Journal of Legal Ethics*, the *South Caroline Law Review* and other publication. In addition to the *Legal Procurement Handbook*, she is also the editor of *Winning Proposals-The Essential Guide for Law Firms and Legal Services Providers* (also available on Amazon).

Silvia is the editor of *The Definitive Guide to Buying Legal Services*.

LinkedIn: https://www.linkedin.com/company/buying-legal-council and https://www.linkedin.com/in/silviahodges/
Twitter: @BuyingLegal and @SilviaHodges
Website: www.buyinglegal.com

Richard Stock, M.A, FCIS, CMC

Richard is the founding partner of Catalyst Consulting. He has been working with lawyers for more than 30 years. His practice is focused on corporate and government law departments. Consulting engagements cover business strategy, workload and workflow protocols, organizational issues, performance and cost management. He has completed more than 500 consulting engagements for law departments, law firms and legal organizations in the U.S., Canada, Europe, the Middle East, and Australia. Richard has negotiated fee agreements with more than 450 law firms on behalf of 80 companies covering more than 125 countries.

Richard authored "Secure Sponsorship," "Scope Legal Services," "Understand Pricing of Legal Services", and "A Step-by-Step Negotiations Process."

LinkedIn: www.linkedin.com/in/richard-stock-a1374a4/
Website: www.catalystlegal.com

Yannis Theile

Yannis works in Bayer's legal department. He previously was the Global Procurement Business Partner for Corporate Legal for M&A, finance/capital markets as well as Antitrust & Investment matters. He focused on appropriate pricing for complex legal matters, taking into account the peculiarities of the different matter types and balancing legal & business aspects in transactions. This was reflected in the choice of legal provider and fee arrangement to deliver the best value while safeguarding good working relationships with legal service providers.

Yannis authored "Quality Management" and contributed to "Performance Management."

LinkedIn: https://linkedin.com/in/yannistheile

Nick Williams

Nick is a highly experienced senior Procurement executive with 25+ year operating experience in the UK, US, and Europe. His strategic business understanding combined with sharp delivery mentality for critical projects in challenging environments drives change in the private and public sector. He is an industry thought leader in Legal Services, regularly invited to speak at Legal/Sourcing events. Nick is Principal Consultant at Proxima and an Advisory Board Member for Thomson Reuters' Legal & Technology Procurement Conferences. Whilst his core focus and passion for change is Legal Services, Nick is also expert in Professional and Financial services procurement.

Nick contributed to "Design a sourcing strategy" and "Performance Management."

LinkedIn: www.linkedin.com/in/nickmwilliams/
Website: www.proximagroup.com

Jason Winmill

Jason is a Partner at Argopoint and has over two decades experience advising corporate legal departments and sourcing organizations. Jason was the "outside architect" and designed the outside counsel partnering program for the country's fifth largest legal department, saving over one hundred million dollars. His legal sourcing approach has been the subject of a Harvard Business School case study. Jason's work has been featured in the WSJ, Corporate Counsel, Law.com, The American Lawyer, Law360, Purchasing Magazine, and Inside Supply Management. He has held positions at Bain & Co. and is a graduate of Harvard College and Harvard Business School.

Jason authored "Assess Firms and Providers."

LinkedIn: www.linkedin.com/in/jason-winmill-71769b2/
Website: www.argopoint.com

Lynsey Wood

Lynsey holds a law degree from Northumbria University and has worked for Coote O'Grady since 2017 following a career as a law firm fee earner. She has a proven track record of achieving significant legal spend savings for Fortune 100 clients across a vast range of industry sectors. As Head of Legal Operations at Coote O'Grady Lynsey manages the legal operations team who help clients reduce their external legal spend through legal invoice review, legal panel reviews and analysis of law firm spend data as well as carrying out negotiations to help clients realize significant cost savings.

Lynsey and Caroline O'Grady authored "Key Performance Indicators and Heat Maps."

LinkedIn: www.linkedin.com/in/uk-legal-invoice-review/ and www.linkedin.com/company/coote-o'grady/
Twitter: @CooteOGrady
Website: www.cooteogrady.com

We thank the following organizations for sharing their expertise and insights:

BTI Consulting Group (www.bticonsulting.com): Chapter "Checklist Cutting Cost & Adding Value."

Elevate (www.elevateservices.com): Chapter "Legal Spend Management."

Lawcadia (www.lawcadia.com): Chapter "A Word About Legal Procurement and Legal Operations."

Wolters Kluwer's ELM Solutions (www.wolterskluwer.com/en/solutions/enterprise-legal-management): Chapter "Checklist Improving Law Firm Performance."

ABBREVIATIONS

AFA	Alternative Fee Arrangement
AI	Artificial Intelligence
ALSP	Alternative Legal Service Provider
CSR	Corporate Social Responsibility
ESG	Environmental, Social and Governance
GC	General Counsel
IP	Intellectual Property
ITT	Invitation to Tender
KPI	Key Performance Indicator
LMSS	Legal Matter Specification Standard
LPM	Legal Project Management
LPO	Legal Process Outsourcing Company
MRA	Master Retention Agreements
MSA	Master Service Agreements
NDA	Non-Disclosure Agreement
PQQ	Pre-Qualification Questionnaire
RFI	Request for Information
RFP	Request for Proposal
RFQ	Request for Quotation
RFT	Request for Tender
SLA	Service Level Agreement
SRM	Supplier Relationship Management
SOW	Scope of Work
T&C	Terms & Conditions
TCO	Total Cost of Ownership
UTBMS	Uniform Task Based Management System

Printed in Great Britain
by Amazon

66638705R00149